The Guitarist's Guide to Composing and Improvising

Jon Damian

Edited by Jonathan Feist

Berklee Press
Director: Dave Kusek
Managing Editor: Debbie Cavalier
Marketing Manager: Ann Thompson
Sr. Writer/Editor: Jonathan Feist
Writer/Editor: Susan Gedutis
Product Manager: Ilene Altman

This book
contains a disc(s)

Do not put through the
machine

ISBN 0-634-01635-0

**berklee
press**

1140 Boylston Street
Boston, MA 02215-3693 USA
(617) 7

DISTRIBUTED BY

HAL•LEONARD®
CORPORATION
7777 W. BLUEMOUND RD. P.O. BOX 13819
MILWAUKEE, WISCONSIN 53213

it Hal Leonard Online at
ww.halleonard.com

D1330457

Table of Contents

CD Tracks

Foreword

In 1975, I had the good fortune to meet Jon Damian. He is one of the few musicians I know who has found his own unique voice and the courage to stay true to it. He has a deep understanding of the history, and, at the same time, is always looking ahead using his fantastic imagination. As my teacher, Jon gave me the confidence to go after my own ideas, and he showed me new ways to look at music. He continues to be an inspiration and example. Now with his new book, *The Guitarist's Guide to Composing and Improvising*, everyone will have a chance to learn about some of the fantastic things in Jon Damian's world.

Music, for me, has always been a place where anything is possible—a refuge, a magical world where anyone can go, all kinds of people can come together, and anything can happen. We are limited only by our imaginations. I believe that what we do and learn inside the world of music can affect what goes on in the world outside in a big, positive way. Music is so important—like food and water. There are so many possibilities, and many doors yet to be opened.

In this book, Jon gives us the keys to open many musical doors. Many of these doors we probably didn't even know were there. The publication of *The Guitarist's Guide to Composing and Improvising* is an important musical event—not just for guitarists, but for all musicians.

There's so much amazing stuff in here.

Bill Frisell

Acknowledgements

Thanks to my wife, Betsy, for her never-ending love and support, to my children, Benjamin and Eugene, for their wonderful ideas, to my mom, Rosie, for her incredible whistling, to my father, Sal, for his artistic support, to my sister, Judy, for her inspiring record collection, to my brother, Butch, for stopping his trumpet lessons, and to bassist, barrister, and consultant, John Voigt, for his friendship and advice.

To all my fellow players for their inspiration, especially my faithful trio members Bob Nieske and Ralph Rosen, to Jim Guttmann for his "fascinatin' rhythm," and to Joel Press and the Press Institute players. To all my colleagues at the Berklee College of Music, to Matt Marvuglio, Larry Baione, and Rick Peckham for their leadership, and to Larry Monroe, Greg Badolato, to Peter Kontrimas and Bob Kroeger for their engineering, and to Berklee Press.

To all my teachers: Al Natale, Bobby "Eyes," Billy Elgart, D. Sharpe, Frank Turziano, Jeronimas Kascinskas, Mr. Barnes, Herb Pomeroy, Gary Burton, Bill Leavitt, to all of the Creative Workshops, and to all the teachers I haven't met yet.

To Jim Hall, Wes, Grant, Kenny, and Django, for their inspiration, to Bill Frisell for his wonderful foreword, Jane Goldman for her insightful quote, to Creative Workshop members Sebastien, Danielle, Apostolos and Henrik for their wonderful playing on *Coronation* and "Mardi Gras," to Tyler for his courage and inspiration, to Ken Barney for Ink Blot research, Peter Boolos for Ivan Pavlov research, Ted Osborne for computer research, Susan Barney for her binding support, and Julie Snow and Bati for their feedback.

And to all of my friends and students, including you, who put up with me.

Introduction

I still remember holding my first guitar, a big old sunburst, acoustic, F hole, Harmony arch top—a $25 chunk of beauty. I remember the excitement of picking out my first chord, and finding where the black dots on those chord diagrams were on the fingerboard. My first major-seventh chord was pure ecstasy. I was like a child turning over rocks to find strange creatures lurking underneath.

I am sure that many of you share this curiosity and excitement. From Bach (yes, Bach played the guitar too!) to Zappa, guitarists have always had one thing in common: curiosity. The guitar provokes curiosity. Just look at it. The guitar can take on very curious shapes and sounds. Just think of what Bach's guitar looked and sounded like, and then think of Zappa's.

Our primary interest may be classical, blues, rock, or jazz. But there is a common bond in all of these musics. They originated as improvisatory ideas. Some curious musician banged around on an instrument (improvised), found an idea he liked, maybe wrote it down (composed), and then shared it with others. Gradually, a musical style was born. The most exciting part of playing any music is during these periods of improvisation (at least, in my experience).

What is improvisation? This works for me: "Improvisation consists of the ability to be aware of a moment (in this case, a musical one) and react to it in an efficient manner." This actually holds true for the art of composition, as well, since composition is an extended improvisation. Since it is tough for me to separate the two, I use the word "comprovisation."

For centuries, the guitar has been a wonderful machine for comprovisation, described as "a little orchestra" by various folks, including Beethoven and Berlioz. As soloists, playing this incredible little orchestra, we can sound a single note in many different tone colors. We can add more notes to create a melody, join this melody in counterpoint with another melody or two, accompany this counterpoint with a percussive tap on the body, add a choir of full 5- or 6-note chords, and—wow, we sure have a lot to work with!

The following is a collection of resources for the curious guitarist. This collection challenges guitarists of all styles and levels to expand their creative resources for improvising and composing on the guitar. A world of possibilities will open for you to bring to your music. If things at first sound too intellectual, always remember that something that you now do "instinctively" on the guitar—like playing a favorite chord—was once an intellectual procedure to play. You had to look at those dots on the chord diagram, find them on the fingerboard with your fingers, and hope for the best. But now, playing that chord is as instinctive to you as scratching your head!

The ideas presented here are intended as catalysts to stimulate creative thought. Many of the ideas are long-range concepts that will always be developing within our curious selves.

After more than thirty years, the most fascinating aspect of the guitar is its ability to surprise me with possibilities. The guitar can whisper or shout, sound warmly sweet, scream with a metal edge, be tapped like a drum, sing a simple song, or become a choir of two to six contrapuntal voices, serenading its conductor: you.

This book is intended as a refreshing source for musical ideas that help the guitarist develop as an improviser and composer. I hope that it stimulates and inspires you to search for the guitar's endless musical treasures.

Getting Around

As all the elements of a musical sound are interdependent, so too are all the chapters and topics in this book interconnected. When a musical sound is produced, there is complete presence of loudness or softness, tone color, rhythm, direction, pitch, shape, and texture. When improvising and composing, an ability to react to all these elements adds to our creative resources. Since all music contains these elements, guitarists of all levels and idiomatic interests will find these pages helpful.

Each chapter begins with studies that are accessible to all levels. As each chapter progresses, its studies become more advanced. If an unknown technique or question arises—for example, concerning a scale or an interval—you may wish to flip to chapter 6, "Foundations." This chapter is a collection of study and reference materials, and it will help you progress deeper into the earlier chapters.

Even if you are an advanced player, try *all* the ideas in this book. The most basic sounding/looking concept may surprise you with its challenge. Also, the more advanced studies will bring an awareness of the importance of fundamentals.

Before continuing into the rest of the book check out the "Notation Symbols" page that follows these opening pages. Also, in case of an emergency, refer to the "Incredible Time Machine Study" at the end of chapter 6.

Here is a brief summary of each chapter:

Chapter 1: The Basic Sound Dimensions. This chapter contains improvisation and awareness studies in dynamics, rhythm, direction, and articulation. These are the essential height, width, depth, and shape producers behind our musical ideas.

Chapter 2: The Single Note Line. This chapter includes ideas for developing a single note line for tune improvisation and composition. The "Palette Chart," detailed in chapter 4, is introduced here. Tunes inspired by these techniques are included for study and play along.

Chapter 3: Counterpoint. Included here is use of canon in a modal improvisation, simple counterpoint etudes, counterpoint techniques for improvisation of standard tune progressions, the counterpoint diary, and a continuation of counterpoint topics introduced in chapter 2. Compositions and examples inspired by these contrapuntal techniques are included for study and play along.

Chapter 4: 3-Note Structures—The Palette Chart. The Palette Chart is explained in detail. This chart serves as a directory for studies in 3-note structures. Techniques are presented for quartal voicings, cluster voicings, and independent voice motion in 3-note structures. Tunes and examples focusing on Palette Chart concepts are used for study and play along.

Chapter 5: Form—Putting It All Together. Extending ideas over an overall form is a challenge. Forms are introduced with suggestions on how to build your own.

Chapter 6: Foundations. This chapter contains scale studies, ear studies, interval and arpeggio studies, reference sheets and templates, a bibliography, crossword puzzle, and the Incredible Time Machine Study.

Please enjoy the book. I have introduced these studies to guitarists of many musical persuasions—rock, funk, jazz, and classical—and have heard some amazing, creative adaptations. The most important thing is to write etudes from the ideas presented here. By writing, you push an idea deeper into your musical belly. Send me some of your own inspirations. I would love to hear them.

Notation Symbols

The following symbols are used throughout *The Guitarist's Guide to Composing and Improvising.* Traditional guitar notation symbols are shown here, as are some new ones, for which no traditional symbol exists.

String Indications

Circled numbers traditionally indicate strings.

① indicates the high E string.
② indicates the B string.
③ indicates the G string.
④ indicates the D string.
⑤ indicates the A string.
⑥ indicates the low E string.
° indicates an open string.

Finger Indications

Numbers without circles traditionally indicate fingerboard-hand fingering.

1 indicates the index finger.
2 indicates the middle finger.
3 indicates the ring finger.
4 indicates the pinky.

Position Indications

Fingerboard positions may be indicated in Roman numerals above the staff.

III indicates third position.

Interval Indications

Boxed numbers indicate pitch intervals.

2 indicates an interval of a second.

3 indicates an interval of a third.

24 indicates an interval of a second and a fourth.

Specific quality of intervals are indicated as follows.

Maj. indicates major (Maj7 indicates a major seventh).

– (dash) indicates minor (–2 indicates a minor second).

+, ♯, or Aug. indicates augmented (♯5 indicates an augmented fifth).

° or Dim. indicates diminished (°5 indicates a diminished fifth).

P. or Perf. indicates perfect (P. 5 indicates a perfect fifth).

Direction Indications

Counterpoint and melodic development examples use the following symbols:

indicates an ascending line.

indicates a descending line.

indicates upward-contrapuntal or compound-similar lines.

indicates downward-contrapuntal or compound-similar lines.

or indicates oblique direction (one line stays the same, the other moves).

or indicates contrary direction (lines approach or leave each other).

About the CD

Enclosed with *The Guitarist's Guide to Composing and Improvising*, you will find a one-hour CD consisting of eighty tracks that will add a sound perspective for study, observation, and play-along. The CD begins with an A-natural tuning note and then moves chronologically with the book, providing sound illustrations of many of the musical examples.

There are tracks that are etudes—studies focusing on one topic, such as clusters or a particular counterpoint technique. There are also shorter listening examples, illustrating the II-V-Is of Life, or perhaps some of the Palette Chart Family seeds. There are interactive play-along tracks for improvisation and even a Musical Rorschach Test! Finally, there are full compositions that illustrate the bringing together of concepts discussed throughout the book.

All tracks are meant for your study, both as an observer and as a performer. Study the text first, then listen to its accompanying illustration. Observe with your ears, then learn to play the illustration with the help of the CD. In this process, you will bring the concept to musical life and develop a deeper understanding.

Most importantly, use these ideas in your creative musical life as improviser and composer, to feed your hopefully never-ending curiosity.

Chapter 1   The Basic Sound Dimensions

I am sure we all remember math class when the teacher introduced us to geometry. Remember trying to draw all those rectangles, cubes, triangles, and trapezoids? Figuring out their heights, widths, and depths? The artist in me enjoyed the drawing part of the math class, but the math part of it left me in the dust. So, I gravitated toward the arts, primarily music and learning the guitar. I thought I was safe from the math classes of the world, until I realized that the world of music art had its own dimensions of height, width, and depth!

I guess that I was so absorbed in learning all those pretty chords and licks that I was blind (and deaf) to how the basic sound dimensions could help my playing and composition. It was a combination of folks—my first art teacher, Mr. Barnes; the master guitarist, Jim Hall; my composition teacher, Jeronimas Kacinskas; and a screaming (at me) conductor (not to be named here)—who, together, showed me how a close awareness and control of the basic sound dimensions could inspire my performance, improvisation, and composing abilities. I realized that all those nice chords and licks I was using could be a *lot* nicer and more powerful if I shaped them with the basic sound dimensions. Let's look at the dimensions in order of importance (from my present perspective).

1. **Dynamics.** How loud or soft the musical idea is, and a respect for silence. This is the sound dimension that creates *depth* in music—how *close* the music is to the listener.

2. **Rhythm.** How long or short the musical idea is, and a respect for the silence between the ideas. Rhythm creates the *width* of the music—its horizontal or time dimension.

3. **Direction.** Is the musical idea going up, down, or staying the same? The direction dimension creates the *height* or contour of the musical idea. When two melodies are sounded in counterpoint, or two players are improvising simultaneously, awareness of their basic direction relationship is of prime importance.

4. **Articulation.** How sharp or how round sounding the musical idea is. The manner of attack or articulation of our pick and/or fingers creates the musical idea's basic *shape* and tone color.

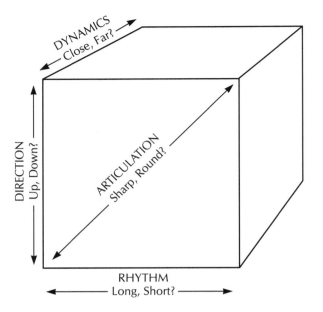

Fig. 1.1. The Basic Sound Dimensions

We are already masters of the use of the sound dimensions in our most basic music communication: our spoken language. Each of us has a unique way of speaking, shaped by how loud or how soft we talk, how fast or how slow we talk, the direction or how we move up and down with our talking, and of course, how we attack our words, our articulation. How we use these elements gives us our "talking personality." Of course, the words we use are important also. But we all use the same words. It is the delivery of these words—their loudness, rhythm, direction, and articulation—that produces the personality of our speaking.

In the study of music improvisation and composition, the many intellectual and mathematical concepts (such as scales, intervals, arpeggios, B♭Maj7, flat nine, sharp this, sharp that) are enough to drive us crazy. Of course, these intellectual ideas are like the "words" of our musical language. They are necessary and important to have and understand, but they don't come to musical life without an awareness of the basic sound dimensions.

When we are speaking, we are improvising and interacting. If we could respond as closely in our musical improvisation as we do in our everyday use of language, it would be a great help in our playing.

We cannot play music without including the basic sound dimensions. They happen automatically. But how aware of them are we? And what level of control do we have with them?

This chapter presents techniques and pieces of music that will inspire your playing and composing by developing your awareness of the basic sound dimensions. Some of the studies may seem quite unique. This is a good thing. That light of awareness may just pop on, thanks to your curiosity. Have fun with these ideas.

This chapter may even improve your math!

"Don't play what's there,

play what's not there."

—Miles Davis

Dynamics: How Loud, How Soft, How Silent, How Close?

Our greatest teachers seem to appear from anywhere. They are the folks who bring about an awareness of the musical areas that need our attention. These teaching moments can happen at any time, and sometimes, they can be painful.

Once, at a rehearsal, a conductor let me have it. "Guitar player, you're too loud. Turn down!" I was very embarrassed, but I learned an important lesson: Playing the "right notes" means playing the correct dynamic level, as well.

Awareness and respect for silence is a hard lesson for guitarists because breathing—such an important factor for other instrumentalists—is not an issue. In saxophones, trumpets, flutes, and all the other wind instruments in the world, there is a built in silence producer: having to take a breath. Not withstanding circular breathing (a difficult technique in which some wind players, and thankfully not many, can play an unbroken length of sound by sneaking in a breath somehow), wind players have a natural respect for silence. With wind instruments in mind, let's try something. You'll need your guitar for this.

The Wind Guitar

Imagine that you are a wind player needing to breathe for survival. Play anything you wish, but as you are playing, exhale as if you were producing the sounds with your mouth.

If you stop playing, breathe in. Play as long an idea as you wish, but when you have to take a breath, stop playing. Continue for a while. Do you find that you are using silence in places you had never thought of before? Good. The silences created as you breathe give your ideas clear beginnings and endings, helping the listener follow them better. Just think what our spoken language would be like if we had no need to breathe. Endless chatter would take on new dimensions. Singing while you play (a la Keith Jarrett, George Benson, et al) is a technique that emulates a wind player's phrasing. Try scatting also.

Exploring Dynamic Range

Guitarists are actually more fortunate then most wind players when it comes to the power of dynamics. Our dynamic range—how soft to how loud we can play—is incredibly wide. The guitar can whisper, it can roar.

Play any *one* note on the guitar. Make it whisper, make it roar. Find all the dynamic points in between. Slowly bring it down to silence. Then, add a second note. Explore how many ways you can explore dynamics with these two notes. Add a third note, if you wish. Play something you have played hundreds of times, but now explore it with your new dynamic range. Get dramatic!

Let's put silence to work for us in another way: as an improvisational and compositional tool. I call this next technique *Fireworks!*

Fireworks!

Picture a fireworks display. There is a brilliant spray of colors. Then, bit by bit, the colors fall and fade, leaving the black sky ready for another splash of excitement.

Now, let's create a musical fireworks display. Notes will be the fireworks, and silences will be the black sky.

Play or sing any simple musical idea. For now, use three notes of a major scale (use any rhythm). Later, try *Fireworks!* using any musical idea you wish.

Do   Re   Mi

Play or sing this again but replace Do with silence.

Re   Mi

Play or sing it again but replace Re with silence.

Mi

Then replace Mi with silence.

Repeat this routine, letting it flow with no apparent seams in the "Do Re Mi" idea. Here is a simple 4-bar example that passes twice through "Do Re Mi." I beefed up the line with some double stops (two notes played at the same time) and a chord (3-note voicing).

Fig. 1.2. Do Re Mi with Fireworks!

As you can see, *Fireworks!* is a fun way to create new ideas from old ones. It could also be used to extend a new idea, using the development process called *extraction* (adding silence). Generally, development is thought of as an additive process, but extraction also works great.

Try other variations as well. Expand *Fireworks!* to include more notes. Challenge yourself.

Also try *Fireworks!* with one of those tired licks of yours, and see what happens. You can develop new licks from the old by tapping into the power of silence.

Here is an example that takes a 2-bar *motif* (idea) from the bebop language. The motif is expanded into an 8-bar phrase by repeating it three times. On each repetition, some notes are extracted (replaced with silence). It plays over "rhythm changes"—the standard jazz chord progression drawn from George Gershwin's classic, "I Got Rhythm."

Asterisks (*) indicate extracted notes.

Fireworks! With a Bebop Motif
Over Rhythm Changes in F

Fig. 1.3. Fireworks! with a Bebop Motif

As this example shows, you can add silence wherever you wish. I removed up to three notes on some bars.

Here is an example of a 1-bar chord comping (accompaniment) idea followed by *Fireworks!* variations of the first bar. Try to keep it going. Write in some more variations.

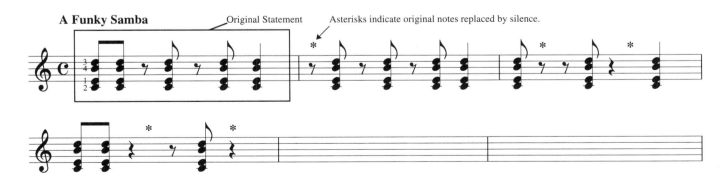

Fig. 1.4. Fireworks! and Comping

Write and play your own variations.

Try *Fireworks!* without your guitar. Use your voice as an instrument.

AND	**TRY**	**IT**	**WITH**	**WORDS**
	TRY	**IT**	**WITH**	**WORDS**
	TRY		**WITH**	**WORDS**
	TRY			**WORDS**
	TRY			

You don't have to be mechanically perfect in adding silence—especially when improvising. Everyone feels their own manner of adding silence. Be patient. A combination of writing out and improvising *Fireworks!* ideas will eventually help this technique to become a natural (and powerful) part of your improvisation and writing.

My favorite art teacher, Mr. Barnes, taught me another important lesson about silence. One day in a life-drawing class, I was sketching away on a large sheet of newsprint paper, absorbed in the live model who was our subject that day.

Mr. Barnes interrupted me. "Mr. Damian, why is your drawing so small? Do you realize that your drawing is becoming lost on the paper? When you produce an image, be aware of the shape of the image itself, the *positive* space, but also the shape that surrounds the image—the white space or *negative* space. As an artist you must be in touch with both spaces to create a balance in your compositions."

Mr. Barnes then had me hold up my right hand, with my fingers spread. He asked me, "Do you see the shape of your hand?"

"Of course," I responded.

"Do you also see the shape *between and around* your fingers, and how you can change this shape when you move your fingers?"

"Wow," I murmured, as I felt a light turn on inside my head.

A similar light turned on later that day, while I was listening to Miles Davis playing "My Funny Valentine." I realized that Miles was in sensitive touch not only with the melody he was producing (positive space), but also the negative space (piano accompaniment) between the melody notes, which helped him improvise his statement of the melody. I *heard* the balance Mr. Barnes talked about earlier in the day. I began to notice positive space and its "accompanying" negative space everywhere. In the way I talked and spaced my words, feeling the silence between the words and sentences, I realized I had been "composing" and balancing with sound and silence all my spoken life, whenever I communicated with others.

In art class the next day, Mr. Barnes introduced a technique to help us become more visually sensitive to the positive and negative space in our work. The visual art technique is called "scratchboard." In scratchboard, a white paper with a smooth polished surface is blackened with brush and ink, and set to dry. Then, with a sharp object—a pin, for example—the surface is scratched, removing the black ink and exposing the brightness of the paper under the ink. This was the reverse of our sketching technique, which produced dark image on white paper. Mr. Barnes then gave us a scratchboard assignment: create a *black* delicate snowflake. We had to scratch away the negative space to produce our snowflakes. It was a challenge. And Mr. Barnes made his point that day.

Fig. 1.5. Scratchboard

One day a student asked Taiga, "What is the most difficult part of painting?"

Taiga answered,

"The part of the paper where nothing is painted is the most difficult."

—Zen saying

A Sound Scratchboard

In the spirit of Mr. Barnes, let's create a *sound* scratchboard to help us become more aware of music's negative space: silence. Instead of using ink and paper, we will use our guitars and "etch" our sounds into the silence.

First, let's "ink" our musical canvas (cover our silence) with a sustained sound, using a chord, steadily and evenly strummed or plucked. This open-string AMaj7(9) chord will work nicely.

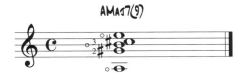
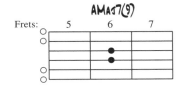

Fig. 1.6. AMaj7(9) chord

Play the chord for a while, smoothly and evenly. Create a nice "covered silence." Then, when you wish, open your mouth and *silently* sing something for a bit. While you "sing the silence," dampen (stop) the chord from sounding. When you are finished singing, close your mouth, and resume playing the chord.

Do you feel the power and presence of the silence space? Continue until you do, and then begin to make your silent singing more active. Eventually, when you dampen the chord, don't use your mouth. See if you have an enhanced sensitivity to the silence space (negative space) that you are creating.

After warming up with a session of Sound Scratchboard, play a familiar single-note melody. Do you feel the silence you are creating around the melody notes? Do you feel the accompaniment the silence gives you? Are you more in touch with the rhythm of your playing and with the interchange of sound and silence?

This chapter on the basic sound dimensions began with a lesson on dynamics. Dynamics is key to observing the other three dimensions—rhythm, direction, and articulation—because they are all shaped by silence. Also, observing our own dynamic level—being able to hear everyone in an ensemble—is key to group improvisation. The ability to hear everyone helps us to respond to them and to support them. It also helps us use their ideas for our own stimulation and support.

Most of all, it helps us to be in the moment. And that is what improvisation is all about.

Rhythm: When, Where?

I had a friend a while back. In fact, he was one of the first folks who inspired me to play the guitar. "Bobby" was his name, a drummer who practiced *all* the time. I could hear his drums from across the street, back in good old Brooklyn, where I was "lowered." I would sit at home with my guitar, enjoying the beauty of its sound, learning its lovely chords. In the distance, I'd hear Bobby, banging away on those drums, and I'd feel sorry for him, that all he had was the smash and crash of his drums. No harmony, no melody. Poor guy.

Then, one day, it was quiet at Bobby's house. Too quiet. I walked over, and went down to his "studio." Through the door, I heard a soft, dry tapping sound.

I slowly opened the door. Bobby, eyes closed, was tapping one stick against the other, incredibly softly and delicately. I watched and listened for almost an hour, until he stopped. He had been completely absorbed (admittedly, so had I). No pretty chords or cool melodies, just this simple dry sound.

Bobby looked up, startled to see me. "Hey man, what's up?" he said.

I told him I didn't hear his tubs (drums) and thought he was dead (chuckles all around).

He said he had been checking out some Afro-Cuban sides (records) and was gassed (excited) at some conga player named Carlos "Patato" Valdez, and how much music he got out of one drum. So Bobby wanted to see how much music he could get out of one stick.

Bobby showed me how he could accompany himself by playing a steady rhythm with the stick for a bit, then answer the steady rhythm with a more syncopated beat. Then, he'd return to the steady rhythm, then back to

"More important than what you played is when you played it."

—Jaan Mondi

syncopation, and so on, creating a dialog. Bobby also showed how he changed the sound of the tapping by holding the stick tighter or looser and changing where he tapped the stick.

"It's like a melody, man, and the other stuff is like counterpoint."

"Sure," I said, with an attitude. "And I guess you can play chords too."

Bobby responded, "Sure, but I need my whole set for that."

Disbelieving, I began to rise to leave, when Bobby said, "Hey man, get your guitar, let's play!"

I responded, tightly, "I've only been playing for about two months. I can't play anything yet."

"Oh, come on," Bobby said, "Of course, you can."

So, I returned with my guitar. Bobby tapped his sticks. I played my guitar, and my first session was off the ground. I soon realized that I could coax some pretty cool "drum" sounds from the guitar, and my first session was a purely rhythmic affair. Bobby returned to his drum set, and in his solos, showed me his "chords" built from combinations of drum colors.

I had no chops (technique) yet, but I could tap, pick, and pluck out some rhythms, and actually had a fun time.

Bobby and I continued our sessions daily. Sometimes we played twice a day. Eventually, I learned to pick out a bluesy melody, which I started to play at each of our sessions. When it came time for me to solo, I returned to my rhythmic ideas. I wasn't hip to licks, arpeggios, and all that jazz yet.

After a while, as I learned some soloing ideas and chord progressions, I became so absorbed in my new techniques that Bobby noticed, and he mentioned that I was losing my rhythmic groove. I felt badly and thought I was a failure. But then I realized that my "rhythmic focus" was being put on the back burner because my concentration was on my newfound chord and solo ideas.

I couldn't be in two places at one time. I didn't want to neglect the rhythmic awareness I had developed, so I tried to balance my practice sessions at home with pure rhythmic improvisations, almost like I was a drummer. I would mute (dampen) my strings, and play along with records purely rhythmically.

Eventually, as my ear became stronger and more confident, I began to put some pitches to the rhythms. Slowly, things felt better. I learned that if I simplified a melody, I could concentrate more on the rhythmic groove. Thanks to Bobby, I had started thinking like a drummer. Today, about thirty-five years later, I am still working on keeping a rhythmic groove, and I am still inspired by those early sessions. In fact, I still practice my guitar as a drum.

Two questions I am often asked are, "How can I improve my chord playing and comping (accompaniment) ability?" and "I am bored with my single-note ideas, where can I find new ones?"

Finding new chord and single-note ideas—for example, in a book like this—would give us *more* to work with. But as the opening quotation says, "More important than *what* you play is *when* you play it." I have found the key to helping any idea work better, whether it be a really hip voicing, a single-note idea, or a funny joke, is *timing:* reacting to a moment, rhythmically. Rhythm is an integral part of our everyday life. It is a powerful communicator in our speaking and the way we walk. It exists in our heartbeats, our breathing, our knocking on a door. We are constantly developing our incredible sense of rhythmic control.

Rhythm is the most intuitive aspect of our improvisation abilities. If I tapped a rhythm—and it needn't be a simple one—and then asked you to tap it back, you probably would be able to do it. If I played a series of notes or chords, not too simple, and asked you to play them back, it would be much more of a challenge. Chords, scales, and other aspects of playing music can require a good deal of study and practice before they become intuitive.

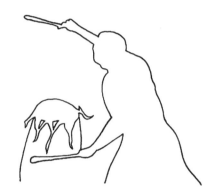

The Guitar in DrumMode

Let's start our rhythmic studies with DrumMode. DrumMode will help you bring your intuitive sense of rhythm into your improvisation. We're going to become percussionists for a while. I developed DrumMode to help increase my rhythmic awareness when playing with other people. By turning my guitar into a "drum," I could isolate rhythm from chords and single-note ideas, and focus more clearly on my goal: rhythmic communication.

To go into DrumMode, dampen your strings with your fingerboard hand. Your pick hand will play normally, but produce percussive sounds on the strings, thanks to your fingerboard hand's muting. Try one string or several strings, depending on whether you wish to focus on playing melody or on comping.

This may feel a little strange at first. It should; you're exploring a purely rhythmic side of the guitar.

DrumMode Exercises

Try these DrumMode exercises. When "GuitarMode" is indicated, play normally, without muting the strings.

1. In DrumMode, play a "drum solo." Imagine a favorite drummer soloing and take off. Explore your innate rhythmic genius! Gradually, you will settle into DrumMode.

2. In DrumMode, play a head (melody) of a technically challenging tune or lick. Then play the same head or lick in GuitarMode. Play small sections of this idea first in DrumMode and then in GuitarMode. Did DrumMode help you notice things that you didn't notice in GuitarMode?

3. In DrumMode, play along with a recording or your favorite radio station. Repeat back the rhythmic ideas you hear from the players. Study the rhythms of each player on the recording—both the soloist and each of the rhythm section players. How deeply can you hear into the rhythms and react to them?

4. In DrumMode, do (3) above, but instead of mimicking the players, improvise your own rhythmic reactions to their playing.

For this next series of DrumMode Studies, you'll work with a tune of your choice. Choose a recording, or better yet, find another guitarist—hopefully, a regular playing partner—to join you. Choose a tune you can play easily, such as a blues tune or a modal progression.

You'll be switching between GuitarMode and DrumMode.

Do each of these exercises twice. First, play a comping part, playing two or more strings in DrumMode. Then, play the melody or solo part, playing just one string in DrumMode. If you are playing with another person, one of you should be the soloist and the other should comp (accompany). Then, switch parts and repeat the exercises.

1. Trading choruses. In GuitarMode, play the tune's first chorus. Play the next chorus in DrumMode, then the next in GuitarMode, and so on, switching every chorus. Did you communicate better rhythmically while in DrumMode? Did you try rhythmic ideas in DrumMode that you wouldn't try in GuitarMode?

2. Trading fours. Start the tune again. Play the *first four* bars in GuitarMode, then the next *four bars* in DrumMode, then the next four bars in GuitarMode, and so on. Any observations?

3. Trading twos. Repeat the above exercise, but switch every *two bars.*

4. Trading bars. Repeat the above exercise, but switch every *bar.*

5. The whole tune. Now play the tune totally in GuitarMode. Any observations?

These exercises should increase the communication level between you and other players. If possible, do these exercises regularly with a playing partner. Invent your own DrumMode exercises.

A Victim of DrumMode

One of my students, who actually became pretty well known on the music scene, once asked me, "Oh sacred one (only kidding), how can I add to my rhythmic ideas? I am really bored with what I use now." I was working with some poets at the time, who I found very inspiring, so I suggested that he use DrumMode to play the rhythms of a poem. I think he found this idea inspiring, since he mentioned it in a *Guitar Player* magazine interview about twelve years later!

Try it with this set of lines from "Kubla Khan" by Samuel Taylor Coleridge.

Kubla Khan

In Xanadu did Kubla Khan

A stately pleasure dome decree

Where Alph, the sacred river, ran

Through caverns measureless to man

Down to a sunless sea.

The Metronome: Friend or Foe?

In the performing arts—theater, dance, comedy, and, of course, music performance—timing is essential. The performer's ability to know when and where things happen is crucial for the clear expression of their ideas. Tempo—an even pulse or beat—is used as an underlying rhythmic guide so that performers can interact together rhythmically. This even pulse, groove, or "center of time" also serves as a point of reference for hearing and appreciating more adventurous rhythms. In music, this pulse can be obvious, not so obvious, or non-existent. As performers, we develop our own *internal* sense of pulse or "center" to ready ourselves for any situation.

In dance, having a strong center of balance is crucial for a safe return from adventurous activity. Dancers practice strengthening and developing this center of balance by working with the *barre* (bar). They use the barre for balance so that they can build muscles in the rest of their body, and develop an awareness of "center."

We musicians have our own version of the barre—the metronome. We use it to help develop our center of time or pulse.

As the dancer's barre is used for support to develop the rest of their body, we will use the metronome to develop our own sense of pulse, and use it as a basic guide. Rather than set it to supply every beat, we will use it to mark groupings, and then fill in the beats ourselves.

The Metronome as Our Barre

For these metronome studies, play a scale of your choice. Later, you may apply these techniques to any music. Set the metronome to 160 beats per minute.

1. Click on beats 1, 2, 3, 4. Play the scale one note per beat or metronome click, "1 2 3 4, 1 2 3 4, etc." This should be easy. If not, have you considered alligator wrestling?

   Follow the gnome for the clicks, hearing one on each beat.

1	2	3	4
CLICK	*CLICK*	*CLICK*	*CLICK*

When you are comfortable playing one note per beat, begin to improvise freely with any rhythms and notes, returning to the basic pattern if necessary.

2. Click on beats 1 and 3. Now, we will *play* at the same tempo (160), but instead of the metronome clicking on each beat (1 2 3 4), we will have it click only two beats per bar, beats 1 and 3. Set the metronome to 80 beats per minute.

   Play the scale, one note per beat, "1 2 3 4, 1 2 3 4, etc.," while the metronome clicks for beat 1 and 3 only. The rest is up to you.

1	2	3	4
CLICK		*CLICK*	

When you are comfortable with this pattern, begin to improvise freely with any rhythms and notes, returning to the basic pattern if necessary.

3. Click on beats 2 and 4. Keep the metronome at 80 beats per minute, but make these clicks on beats 2 and 4.

1	2	3	4
	CLICK		*CLICK*

When you are comfortable with this pattern, begin to improvise freely with any rhythms and notes, returning to the basic pattern if necessary.

Notice that playing with the metronome clicking on beats 2 and 4 feels different than with the click on beats 1 and 3. The 2 and 4 pattern is used to create a "swing feel."

4. Click on beat 1. Now let's have you work a bit harder. Play at the same tempo (160), but have the metronome click for only *one* beat, beat 1. Set the metronome to 40 beats per minute.

Play the scale, one note per beat, "1 2 3 4, 1 2 3 4, etc.," except the metronome clicks beat 1.

1	2	3	4
CLICK			

When you are comfortable with this pattern, begin to improvise freely with any rhythms and notes, returning to the basic pattern if necessary.

5. Click on beat 2. Keep the metronome on 40 beats per minute, but make the click beat 2.

Play the scale one note per beat, "1 2 3 4, 1 2 3 4, etc.," except the metronome clicks for beat 2 only.

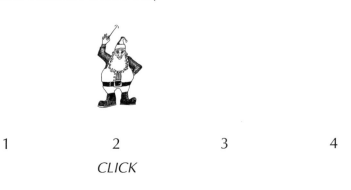

1	2	3	4
	CLICK		

When you are comfortable with this pattern, begin to improvise freely with any rhythms and notes, returning to the basic pattern if necessary.

6. Click on beats 3 or 4. Try making the click only beat 3 or only beat 4. Experiment with other patterns and tempos.

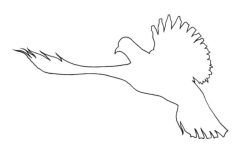

Pulse Study

The Pulse Study focuses on dividing time evenly. Set your metronome to 40 beats per minute.

1. One note per click. Choose a note and play along directly with the metronome, *one note to one click.* If you are using a pick, use alternate picking: down, up, down, up. If you are playing in a finger style, alternate your fingers.

2. Add a visual image. As you play, visualize a cyclic image—a pendulum, the beating of a bird's wings in flight, or any repeating image you choose as your guide through the space of time between clicks.

3. Balance. Practice playing the notes and imagining the cyclic image until you achieve a sense of synchronized balance between your playing, the image, and the metronome.

4. Two notes per click. Keep the metronome at the same setting, and play *two evenly spaced* notes per click. Use your cyclic image to guide you.

5. Three notes per click. When you feel you are "balanced" with the two even notes, the image, and the click, play *three evenly spaced* notes per click.

6. Continue this with three, four, five—all the way up to nine evenly spaced notes per click. Practice each one until they feel balanced.

You are moving up a rhythmic scale. Like the notes of a pitch scale, each point of the rhythmic scale has its own personality, which you will begin to recognize. As you will notice, some divisions are easier than others.

7. Come back down. Now work your way back down the rhythmic scale: 9, 8, 7, 6, 5, 4, 3, 2, 1. It takes time to get used to this routine, but the time devoted will really help you feel the divisions naturally.

8. Leaps. Try leaping around the rhythmic scale. For example play 3, then 7, then 2, then 6, and so on. Change on every beat.

9. Variations. Begin to vary the notes. Also, try giving some notes accents (playing a note louder than the others) to challenge your "center of time balance." Try replacing some of the beats with silence (extraction).

The Magical Clap Study

Playing percussion instruments, or clapping, is like dancing. Making our entire body a rhythm instrument through dancing, clapping, DrumMode, or playing a percussion instrument, is a great way to help our sense of time balance. The final study in this section combines dancing with playing one of the most ancient of percussion instruments: our hands. It is called The Magical Clap Study.

This one is simple.

1. Set your metronome to any tempo.

2. Clap your hands with the metronome until you can make the sound of the clicks disappear. It sounds easy, but it is tricky.

3. How many *consecutive* clicks can you make disappear with your claps? The record presently stands at 41. Beat it!

Admire the rhythms around you, and learn from them. From the rhythmic ingenuity of Thelonious Monk tunes, to the rhythms in children's voices, to the click-clack of those wiper blades accompanying your own ingenious tapping on the steering wheel, rhythmic ideas are everywhere.

"What goes up..."

—Djinn Aa-Om

Direction: Up, Down, The Same?

In Dynamics and Rhythm, we focused on communication in an ensemble. As an accompanist, good communication skills strengthen our ability to support a soloist. As a soloist, they help us draw ideas from those supporting us. In this section, we will add another dimension of awareness: Direction. Is the music going up, down, or staying the same? How can an awareness of direction inspire and strengthen our improvisation and composition ideas?

The study of counterpoint explores the direction relationship between two single-note lines (melodies). Are the two lines moving along together in the same direction? This is called *similar* motion. Are the two lines moving toward each other or away from each other? This is *contrary* motion. Or is one line staying the same as the other line moves up or down? This is called *oblique* motion.

These interactive direction possibilities, of course, always exist when two or more things are happening. Imagine an ice skating duo as moving in "counterpoint" to each other.

We will look at some compositions that use direction as their principal developmental component. Also, we will see how in playing in an ensemble, we actually become a line of direction counterpoint, moving against the other players. An awareness of this relationship adds to our improvisational resources.

Contrary motion is considered one of the strongest motions since it creates the most independence between the two lines or ideas. Imagine those ice skaters as they separate in opposite directions and then speedily come together to do a ferocious twirl and then move apart again to come back together for an even more ferocious twirl, then a toss in the air! Ouch!!

Let's see how to utilize direction to inspire your writing and improvisation.

Direction as a Compositional Resource

I have found that composing, or "writing improvisation," has helped the performance or "playing improvisation" side of my musical life. When composing, I can take more time to work and study ideas that haven't become part of my regular playing improv skills yet. It is a great way to explore new ideas. Plus you end up with some of your own tunes!

I wrote the tune "Skee-Dap-M-Be-Bap" (fig. 1.7) to help strengthen my awareness of direction. It started out as a simple bluesy melodic line (see bars 1 through 4) for two guitars, and focuses on contrary motion between the two lines. We'll call this piece an "etude" (pronounced EH-TOOD-AH, with a holier-than-thou attitude), which sounds extremely impressive.

The line repeats (bars 8 through 11), then returns, transposed up a fourth (bar 13) with some variations. The line returns in its original form (bar 22). The tune ends with a tag (bar 25).

For the second guitar, instead of using a standard blues chord progression, I wrote a specific line, which gives me more control over how the tune will be played. I predominantly use contrary motion between guitar 1 and guitar 2. The arrows in fig. 1.7 indicate the directions of the lines. The contrary motion between the lines gives them strength and independence, which I prefer to a more static chordal accompaniment. In bars 4 through 7, 11 through 12, and 17 through 21, the dynamics come down to soft, and I use oblique motion between the lines to create even more contrast.

For the improvisation section, follow an *extended* 12-bar form. *Extended* simply means that each chord lasts twice as long as in a usual 12-bar form, so the form is actually twenty-four bars long. Also, contrary motion should be maintained between the soloist and accompanists.

The direction dimension helped in the composition of this tune. It becomes a powerful idea for its players during the improv section.

Fig. 1.7. Skee-Dap-M-Be-Bap

Skee-Dap-M-Be-Bap

For Two Guitars

Here is an example from a solo guitar piece, composed for my new young friend, Juliette. Contrary motion is used in the ending for one of the piece's sections. Notice how contrary motion helps bring out the guitar's different tone colors in each line.

For Juliette
A Contrary-Motion Example

Fig. 1.8. "For Juliette" Excerpt

Direction as an Improvisation Resource

In the Creative Workshop ensemble, an improvisatory new-music group at Berklee College of Music, I often give the performers direction indications to shape their improvisations. An improvisatory work entitled *The Coronation*, composed for six guitars, opens with a guitar quartet (the peasants). In cue 2 of the excerpt below, a Bach-like 4-part chorale is improvised in E minor. Two guitarists improvise contrary-motion lines to each other. The other two guitarists then improvise direction canons (an echo-like repetition of the other players' directions) in answer, a bar later.

Below is an excerpt of the score and a recording (track 6) of the workshop improvising on cues 1 and 2—the section leading up to the king's entrance (well it is a coronation you know!). The next track (track 7) is of a later section of *The Coronation* when the quartet breaks into duos and improvises in double time, using the same direction parameters. What you are hearing is *totally* improvised by the workshop. I think they sound great. Thanks Apostolos, Danielle, Henrik, and Sebastien!

⫘ The Coronation ⫘
An Improvisatory Work for Six Guitars

Accompanists 1 (two players): Peasants

Accompanists 2 (two players): Peasants

Soloist 1: The King

Soloist 2: The Queen

Introduction

Cue 1

Accompanists 1 and Accompanists 2 begin even quarter notes in adagio tempo (quarter note equals 60 beats per minute) in E minor.

Imagine the interior of a large sunlit sixteenth-century cathedral.

Cue 2

Accompanists 1 begin to introduce occasional eighth notes.

Improvise in direct (at the same time) contrary motion to each other.

In E minor until Cue 3

At the same time, Accompanists 2 begin to introduce occasional eighth notes.

Improvise in direction canon at the bar motion to each other.

In E minor until Cue 3

Cue 3

Entrance of Themes

At King's entrance

Accompanists 1 and 2 move to E major and muted strings

If you would like the rest of the score for study or performance, please write to me!

Now you try it!

I hope you enjoyed the workshop's improvisations. Now, try a direction improvisation yourself. In the Direction Study below, I have written sixteen bars (eight bars repeated) in E minor, similar to one of the lines played in *The Coronation*. Try playing along with this line. Here are four ideas; try *all* four ideas, in any order you wish! Also, try improvising and writing lines that move in similar and oblique motion to the line in the example.

1. *Improvise* in E minor along with the CD (track 8), moving in *contrary* motion to the line (try a few takes). You can improv above or below the original line or a little of each.

2. *Compose* (write) a line in the blank staff (or several variations on your own paper) in E minor, moving in *contrary* motion to the line. Then *play* the line along with the CD track. You can write above or below the original line or a little of each.

3. *Improvise* with the Direction Study, moving in *direction canon* (play a similar direction idea a bar later). You can play above or below the original line or a little of each.

4. *Compose* (write) a line in the blank staff (or several variations on your own paper) in *direction* canon. Then play the line with the CD track. You can write above or below the original line or a little of each.

Direction Study

Fig. 1.9. Direction Study

Now with a Blues!

I hope you enjoyed tapping the power of direction motion. Now that you are getting accustomed to using direction as an improv possibility, try the same four ideas but this time over a G-blues bass line. Write them in the top staff.

G-Blues Direction Study

Fig. 1.10. G Blues Direction Study

Again, the possibilities are endless. In any tune, try playing a chordal accompaniment that explores various direction possibilities against the tune's melody or improv solo. It takes a new level of concentration but it is worth it.

Mime Study

Before moving onto Articulation, I would like to introduce you to another improvisatory technique, which combines the study of rhythm and direction. This study is called Mime Study. It helps strengthen rhythmic and direction communication between members of an ensemble. First, let's try it with a small ensemble: just you and your stereo. Later, you should try this with a human partner or ensemble. It is much more rewarding and interesting to play with real people.

Choose any recording—preferably one with which you are unfamiliar. While it plays, you play the music's rhythm and direction ideas as closely as possible, but *don't make a sound!* The recording should be the only sound you hear. Move your hands *near* your guitar, matching (miming) the recording's rhythms and direction motion. Focus on "becoming" the recording.

Continue this for several minutes. After a while, ESP or "extrasensory" perception develops.

Eventually, begin to introduce actual sounds until you are playing constantly.

When you do mime study with another musician, have them play a *solo* improvisation of their choice. Anything goes. This person should be the *only* person actually playing, while you mime their rhythms and direction motion. After your partner is finished, switch roles; *you* take a solo improvisation of your choice. Anything goes. Your partner now plays *silently,* following your rhythmic and direction ideas as closely as possible.

Continue in this cycle for several rounds. Eventually, the "silent partner" should gradually begin to introduce actual sounds until both you and your partner are playing constantly.

By this point, your "ESP" should be warmed up.

Mime Study is a powerful concert piece, since it is visually quite captivating for an audience. Try it with a larger ensemble as well. I use it regularly with the Creative Workshop to tune up the communication levels. It is a great way to kick off a rehearsal. As you did with just one partner, pass the solo around, with the rest of the band miming whoever is soloing. After each player has soloed, begin with solos again, but this round, gradually introduce actual sounds until the entire ensemble is playing constantly.

Of course, this requires players who are willing to take a chance and truly improvise in the moment.

I hope these ideas help you utilize the power of the direction dimension. We will continue to explore direction throughout the book, especially in the Counterpoint, Single Note, and Palette Chart chapters. Now, let us move onto the final section of chapter 1, which is another fascinating sound dimension: articulation, the manner of musical speaking.

Articulation: Sharp Sound, Round Sound

"Articulate: Endowed with the power of speech"

—The American Heritage Dictionary

It was during my travels in the Far East and Asia that I met two incredible instruments: the shamisen and the ch'in. The *shamisen,* which I met on the island of Okinawa, is a Japanese guitar-like instrument whose body consists of, for resonance purposes, the skin of a habu stretched over a wooden frame (a *habu* is a deadly snake, a pit viper). The fingerboard is fretless, its three strings are made of silk, and it is plucked with a long plectrum made of ivory. The *ch'in,* a seven-string Chinese lute, is played with fingers. Both of these instruments amazed me in the richness of their articulation—how the players could "speak" with their instruments through a seemingly endless variety of ways to strike, pluck, pull, and snap the strings. The repertoire of tone colors produced from the shamisen and the ch'in was remarkable. I discovered later, after some research, that the ch'in has approximately 150 ways of striking the strings, and each has its own name!

At first, I wondered why the guitar world didn't have this awareness, this thirst for a variety of articulation and tone color. After more research, I discovered that some of our great nineteenth-century guitar-playing ancestors were deeply exploring the timbral (tone color) possibilities of the guitar. Fernando Sor's *Method for the Spanish Guitar,* written in 1830, has detailed descriptions for imitating various orchestral instruments, such as trumpet, flute, French horn, and oboe. In *A Modern Method for the Guitar: The School of Francisco Tarrega,* written by his student, Pascual Roch, there are descriptions for achieving drum sounds, bell sounds, the hoarse voice of an old man or woman, and even crying sounds.

A friend, a classical guitarist, told me of a contemporary work composed for solo guitar that rivals the articulation complexities of the ch'in. The work is titled *Las Seis Cuerdas (The Six Strings),* composed by Alvaro Company in 1963. In the piece the composer has invented his own pick-hand notation. A line ——————— represents the string section from the twelfth position (fret) to the bridge of the guitar.

Fig. 1.11. Alvaro Company's Guitar Diagram

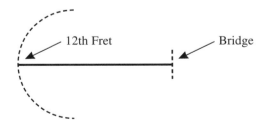

The symbol ∏ represents the player's fingernail. Bringing the symbols together tells the player at a glance where to strike the string, and the angle of striking.

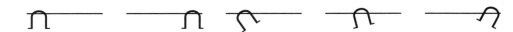

Fig. 1.12. Alvaro Company's Articulation Diagrams

In *Las Seis Cuerdas,* each note has a different attack!

It is inspiring for me to learn about guitarists who explore one of the instrument's great assets: its infinite array of tone-color possibilities.

The Jazz and Blues Lyric School

How many times have we seen the word "lyrical" used to describe a performance? From my perspective, the term *lyrical* refers to how a player emulates the tone colors of language—our most basic sound communication—through their articulation with their instruments. The jazz and blues legends truly spoke through their axes (instruments), from the slide guitars of Blind Willie Johnson and Robert Johnson to the horns of Miles Davis, Lester Young, and Sonny Rollins, to the innovations of Jimi Hendrix.

They were inspired by one of the most ancient of musical instruments: the human voice. Many of the players sang and/or worked with singers. In the jazz idiom, many of the tunes the players chose to blow (improvise) over were originally *heard* and *sung* over the radio or at the movies. These tunes were Top 40 popular tunes! "All The Things You Are" was on *Your Hit Parade* for eleven weeks, twice in the #1 position! These tunes were consistently heard, *sung to,* and danced to by lots of folks. When the cats (players) played these tunes, they were quite familiar with the lyric content. The wonderful jazz dictionary, *A Jazz Lexicon,* by Robert S. Gold, is a testament to the blues and jazz players' love of language.

I guess I am from the lyric school. I would rather learn tunes from recordings of singers than from anywhere else. It helps me in my playing to think less about *what* notes to "speak" but *how* to "speak" them.

Language can be inspiring, and we can use it to explore tone colors on the guitar. At first I was overwhelmed by the possibilities. Since there is no tone color "scale" to help my studies, I devised my own. Other folks who have tried this idea have added to their tone color range. It is called "Alphabet Study."

Alphabet Study

The tone color scale we will use is a simple one: the alphabet. Observe as you speak the alphabet, "A, B, C...." Note the twenty-six tone colors your mouth produces, how they are produced, and the movement of your lips, tongue, and teeth. Incredible!

Now, with your pick hand (using a pick or your fingers), try to produce these twenty-six sounds—or at least some facsimile of them—on your guitar.

Choose a single note for your fingerboard hand to hold during this exploration. Imagine the sound of the letter A. Then with your pick hand, play the note until you find an articulation that sounds similar. Try varying the angle of the pick or your fingernail, or the location on the string that you are playing (between bridge and fingerboard), to find the sound. When you have your first tone color for the letter A, move on to the letter B. Just as your mouth changes to speak these letters, your pick hand should change to play them. How does your hand feel when you play the letter B, relative to how you played the letter A? More angle? Nearer to the fingerboard? Continue through the rest of the alphabet.

If this seems crazy, that's because it is! But! If you try it, I promise you will find some interesting sounds.

This is a subjective study. Everyone will play their tone color alphabet differently. It is simply a study to explore an array of tone color possibilities.

I found a sheet in my file from a student, a while back, who actually wrote out his own ideas of how to "speak" his tone color alphabet. Here it is. Some of his indications sound like James Bond ordering a drink.

I think it's fun seeing someone else's approach to this study.

A   **Straight pick, medium pressure, medium deep between front and middle pickup.**

B   **Further back with some twist, some body, medium deep.**

C   **Above middle pickup, more pressure, more twist, thin shallow.**

D   **Above middle pickup, pressure as "C," twist, slightly more body.**

E   **Quite thin, high pressure, twist, right behind middle pickup.**

F   **Low pressure, medium body, little attack, no twist.**

G   **Some twist, some attack, some body, between middle and front pickup.**

H Low pressure, no twist, much body, pure deep, between front and middle pickups.

I High pressure over middle pickup, just the tip, no twist.

J As "I" but with twist.

K Medium deep, high pressure, some twist, between front and middle pickups.

L Low pressure, above front pickup, no twist, deep.

M Low pressure, between neck and front pickup, deep, no twist.

N Above front pickup, deep, slight twist, low pressure.

O Between neck and front pickup, low pressure, very deep, very little attack, absolutely no twist.

P Right behind middle pickup, quite thin, medium deep, higher pressure, twist.

Q Very thin, high pressure, twisted, behind middle pickup.

R Tremolo? Above middle pickup, some body, twist, medium pressure.

S Above back pickup, high pressure, just the tip, no twist.

T As "S" but with twist and a bit further back.

U Between front and middle pickup, low pressure, deep, no attack, a tiny twist.

V Above middle pickup, medium deep, big twist, high pressure.

X High pressure, behind back pickup, just the tip, no twist.

Sorry, I don't know where his W, Y, and Z went.

After doing Alphabet Study, try playing the melody of a tune with your new added articulation language. Also, remember the poem earlier in Rhythm? Try "speaking" that poem with your new tone color language. Get your fingerboard hand working also, with note changes, slides, and so on.

Coda: Chapter 1

Before closing this chapter on the basic sound dimensions, I would like to share a final improvisation idea with you. It will draw upon your dynamic, rhythmic, direction, and articulation imaginations, and help you to see why I use conceptual ideas such as DrumMode, Wind Guitar, The Coronation, and Alphabet Study. At first, you may think these studies restrict, but from the illusion of restriction, *new* visions will blossom. So, here is Shamisen Sam.

Shamisen Sam

I would love to give the following improvisation idea to six of my favorite guitarists: (in alphabetical order) Derek Bailey, Bill Frisell, Jim Hall, Wayne Krantz, John Williams, and *YOU*, since you bought this book. I'd record each of you improvising with the following idea, for between 6 and 10 minutes, and then put the six improvisations on a CD! Think about it! So, here goes.

As with the shamisen, you will use only three strings for this improvisation: the high E string (it's the skinniest one!), the B string (the skinny guy's next-door neighbor), and the G string (the B string's neighbor).

The only notes you can play on these strings are the G (third fret) on the high E string, the D (third fret) on the B string, the A note (second fret) of the G string, and, of course, the open strings themselves.

Here are the available notes illustrated on your "shamisen":

Fig. 1.13. Your Shamisen

So, you have six notes. Play them in any order you wish. Explore the dimensions of dynamics, articulation, rhythm, and texture. Besides single-note ideas, improvise using counterpoint, and 2- or 3-note chords. Don't forget harmonics, tapping the guitar as a drum, or any of the other ideas we have been exploring.

Seems restrictive? Give it some time. Let it build. Where and how you build to is totally up to you. Then send me a recording of you in action with Shamisen Sam for the CD!

(Now, I just have to convince Jim, Bill, John, Derek, and Wayne to do it too!)

Chapter 2   The Single-Note Line

YIKES! I just realized I forgot to put another important element in chapter 1, which I hope you have been enjoying, by the way. But I'll just talk about it now. Texture: how *thick,* how *thin* is the music? How many "strands" of single-note lines make up a musical idea? One, two, or many?

Oh, another thing I forgot to tell you. Today, at least right now as I am writing, is actually my birthday! I am lonely sitting here, writing, so *please* sing (or imagine yourself singing) "Happy Birthday" to me. Ready?

HAP-PY BIRTH-DAY TO JON!... HAP-PY BIRTH-DAY TO JON!... HAPPY BI

Thanks! You just sang a single-note line, all by itself. In official music lingo, this is called *monophonic* texture. Now, to continue my spontaneous birthday party, please sing (or again imagine yourself singing) "Happy Birthday," but now, with your favorite choir—let's say the Mormon Tabernacle Choir. Ready? Everybody now!

HAP-PY BIRTH-DAY TO JON!... HAP-PY BIRTH-DAY TO JON!... HAPPY BI

HAP-PY BIRTH-DAY TO JON!... HAP-PY BIRTH-DAY TO JON!... HAPPY BI

HAP-PY BIRTH-DAY TO JON!... HAP-PY BIRTH-DAY TO JON!... HAPPY BI

HAP-PY BIRTH-DAY TO JON!... HAP-PY BIRTH-DAY TO JON!... HAPPY BI

HAP-PY BIRTH-DAY TO JON!... HAP-PY BIRTH-DAY TO JON!... HAPPY BI

HAP-PY BIRTH-DAY TO JON!... HAP-PY BIRTH-DAY TO JON!... HAPPY BI

HAP-PY BIRTH-DAY TO JON!... HAP-PY BIRTH-DAY TO JON!... HAPPY BI

HAP-PY BIRTH-DAY TO JON!... HAP-PY BIRTH-DAY TO JON!... HAPPY BI

HAP-PY BIRTH-DAY TO JON!... HAP-PY BIRTH-DAY TO JON!... HAPPY BI

Good job. That was *lots* of lines (or at least more than one single-note line) moving at the *same* time; this is called a *homophonic* texture. Now, one more time, *please.* Again, with the choir. Except, to add some interest, have each member of the choir start at *a different time,* like a canon. Ready? 1, 2, 3... One at a time now!

HAP-PY BIRTH-DAY TO JON!... HAP-PY BIRTH-DAY TO JON!... HAP-PY

HAP-PY BIRTH-DAY TO JON!... HAP-PY BIRTH-DAY TO JON!

HAP-PY BIRTH-DAY TO JON!... HAP-PY BIRTH-DAY

HAP-PY BIRTH-DAY TO JON!... HAP-PY

HAP-PY BIRTH-DAY TO JON!... HAP

HAP-PY BIRTH-DAY TO JON!

HAP-PY BIRTH-

Beautiful job! Now, that was lots of single-note melodies moving at *different* times, or a *polyphonic* texture. Terms such as "harmony" and "counter-point," of course, also come to mind. These are really by-products of the single-note line, which is the underlying *component* of all the textures. It is the single-note line's magnetic and gravitational powers that keep the music moving, along with rhythm, which is why we are starting with it!

The single-note line has been around for centuries. A single-note idea may very well have been the earliest musical expression. Probably because the early cave people couldn't fit a piano through that tight cave entrance. Picture an early cave: cave mom holds crying cave baby, cave mom instinctively improvises simple song, cave baby stops crying. Cave mom is happy, baby is happy. What made this melody work? Who cares? It worked!

The goal of this chapter is to continue the single-note developments of the early cave people (only kidding, I think) and to add to your single-note creative resources. You will observe *your* single-note ideas as *linear* or *horizontal*, evolving into new ideas, and not only inefficient by-products of chord or harmonic *vertical* thinking. Whether you are creating a single-note line for a composition or working ideas for improvisation, a linear outlook is a more instinctive creative course for melodic development. Language moves in a linear fashion. A sentence begins, and then one word leads to another until the sentence comes to rest. The next sentence begins, inspired by the last sentence, and also comes to rest, much like an unbroken chain of creative energy. In fact, it is much like life—vibrant beings developing each day, the same person we were at birth but now totally different. A lot older!

The studies included in Foundations (chapter 6) will help you learn to *see* and to *hear* scales, intervals, and arpeggios—the important melodic building blocks on the fingerboard. Whatever level guitarist you are, these studies will prepare you for the ideas and studies to come later, so work with them. The first ideas presented in this chapter will be generally accessible, but still a challenge for all levels. We'll gradually move into more sophisticated concepts. As the chapter progresses, I will occasionally remind you about chapter 6, when it may help a particular study.

Have fun with these explorations, and thanks for helping me celebrate my birthday.

The Simplest Melodic Line

Let's begin with the simplest and most beautiful melodic idea: repeating a note. There is strength in repetition; it is the most basic development of an idea. The first single-note study will use only one note—the C-natural on the B string's first fret. Remember Shamisen Sam, when you put your imagination to work with the basic sound dimensions? Now you have only *one* note to work with. (Antonio Carlos Jobim did a pretty good job using this technique in his composition, "One Note Samba.")

Improvise or compose an 8-bar melody using this C with the progression below, "Vamp No. 1" (a *vamp* is a repeated musical idea used as an accompaniment). Find this same pitch elsewhere (the guitar has five of them!) on the fingerboard and use these too. Notice the variety of tone colors the guitar gives you.

The C "works" with the following chord progression, serving as either part of the basic chord or as a tension note (added color). Have fun enjoying how the C sounds as the chords move, and enjoy your improvisation with the sound dimensions.

Vamp No. 1

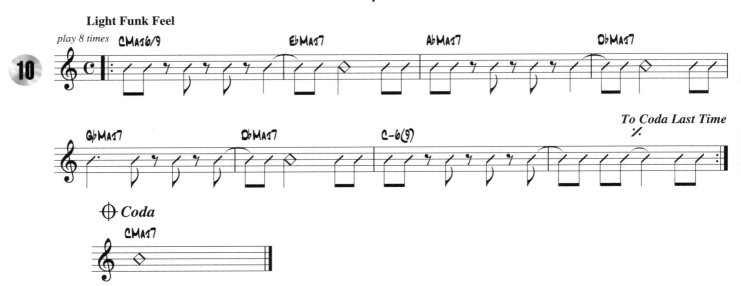

Fig. 2.1. Vamp No. 1. Improvise using only the note C.

Find C on the fingerboard in *all* its octaves. Seeing the octaves of a note (all Cs, in this case) on the fingerboard is an important awareness for playing scales and melodies. The octave is a strong melodic interval, and later in the chapter, we will work with octave adjustment—a really nice way to breathe life into those tired licks! It's also an important interval to learn to *hear*. Check out "Ears 2," a study in Foundations (chapter 6) that will help you learn to hear all the intervals.

Try another improvisation with "Vamp No. 1," using all the Cs on the fingerboard. Choosing a note and then finding all its octaves is a good way to build strong fingerboard observation abilities.

Pitch Motif Studies

Intervals, the distances (up or down) between notes, are the essential building blocks of single-note ideas. An awareness of intervals, with our eyes and ears, helps to describe an idea—also called a *motif*—so it can be repeated. This is the first key in the linear development of a melody for improvisation or composition.

These definitions are from the *American Heritage Dictionary.*

Motif   A recurrent thematic element used in an artistic or literary work. A dominant theme. A short significant phrase. A repeated figure or design in architecture or decoration.

Develop To realize the potentialities of. To cause to expand or grow gradually.

In verbal language, the subject of a sentence may act as a motif, developed in the rest of the sentence. In musical language, development similarly needs a clearly identified motif (a musical "word") to help continue a phrase (sentence) structure. Whether we use single-note ideas to write a tune or to improvise over a chord progression, being able to *continue* an initial idea is an *efficient* way to go. So, respect the ideas you create. Let vertical concepts, such as chord symbols, inspire them, but not interrupt them. Develop your lick—get linear with it, baby!

In the Pitch Motif Studies that follow, we will use 2-note motifs (single intervals) as our building blocks, for now. Eventually, we will use 3-note motifs.

We'll begin with a good old C major scale. Play it anywhere you wish. Eventually, you should work up the following exercises in all keys and types of scales; this is just a warm-up. Remember Foundations (chapter 6) for scale reference, if needed.

First, move intervalically (with intervals) through the scale. From each degree of the scale, play a *diatonic* (from the key) interval. The following shows the C major scale moving in seconds from each scale degree. Then, it moves from each degree in thirds, in fourths, and then fifths, sixths, sevenths, and finally octaves. The "clear" notes indicate the scale notes from which each interval is built.

Let's put them to work. Play the intervals as written. As you can hear, each of them has a distinct personality. Singing the intervals will really help you appreciate their individuality, since your body has to react differently for each distance. (Check out "Ears 2" in Foundations for help with singing and seeing intervals.)

C Major Scale through Diatonic Intervals

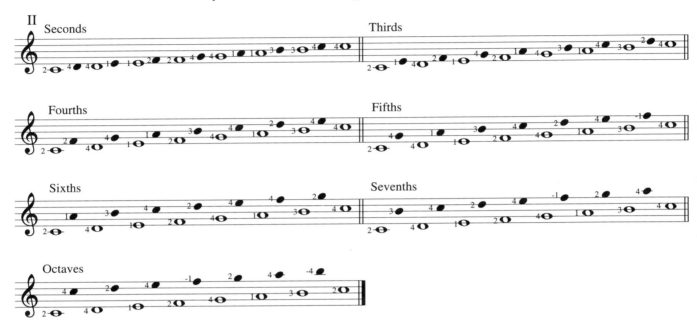

Fig. 2.2. Intervals in C Major

Now, play the intervals over "Vamp No. 2," below. This vamp is a CMaj7(add9) chord moving to CMaj6(add9). Vary the rhythms as you wish, while you play each of the interval scales. Play the intervals down each scale as well. Jump around each interval scale, creating your own designs with the intervals. Make your own vamp tapes for practicing the interval scales.

Play the diatonic intervals over this vamp. Listen for the intervals' colors.

Vamp No. 2

Fig. 2.3. Vamp No. 2

Next is a simple tune composed using primarily thirds. Listen to it being played over "Vamp No. 2." It begins similar to the interval scale studies above, but then occasionally leaps (upward and downward) to new starting notes for the thirds. It also has more rhythmic variety.

This restriction (using only thirds) allows new ideas to blossom. It provides a foundation for further composing and adds to our improvisational possibilities.

In the example below, intervals are indicated using numbers in boxes. You will find similar boxes throughout this book. (Check out the Notation Symbols page in the Introduction for other symbols used in the book.)

Eh-Tood-Ah in Thirds

Fig. 2.4. Eh-Tood-Ah in Thirds

In "Eh-Tood-Ah in Thirds," I used two ideas we looked at in chapter 1: direction contrast and extraction. The first two bars of the melody move upward. As an "answer," and for some contrast, bars 3 and 4 move downward. To complete the 8-bar phrase, bars 5 to 8 basically repeat bars 1 through 4, but are developed using *Fireworks!*—the extraction technique where notes are removed.

Adding Some Spice

In this next example, "approach" notes spice things up a bit. *Approach notes* are notes that come from above or below the "original" melody notes. In bars 1 and 5, notice the F-sharp approach up to the G, and in bar 7, the G-sharp approach to the A. It's up to your taste how much spice you use in your compositions and improvisation.

Eh-Tood-Ah with Spice

Fig. 2.5. Eh-Tood-Ah with Spice

Try writing a study or improvising over this vamp. At first, keep to only one interval, as I did. Then blossom, baby!

Before we continue with more single-note ideas, I would like to make just a couple of points: *melody is harmony* and *catalysts.*

Melody Is Harmony

As you remember from my "birthday party," single-note lines are the "strands" that make up harmonic and counterpoint texture. One single line can also suggest harmony when it moves as an arpeggio or as a melody containing the basic notes *(tones)* of a chord. It is important to recognize these chord tones. To a composer, they can suggest possible harmonic (chordal) accompaniments for a melody. To an improviser playing over a harmonic progression, they can suggest melodic *resting points* (the chord tones) of each chord, and also the *non-resting points* (the non chord tones), since the combination of these notes is what creates melodic life and cadences (movement from non-rest to rest). In "Eh-Tood-Ah with Spice," I wrote the single-note line linearly, repeating the simple third motif. At the same time, I was aware of the relationship of each note to the chord accompaniment, so that I could create the feeling of tension and release (cadence). In bars 3 and 7, notice how the Fs (non-chord tones of C major) create tension as the line passes through them.

In Foundations, there is an arpeggio section for your reference and study. Building an awareness of arpeggios will help with the rest of this chapter, as well as the chapters Counterpoint and 3-Note Voicings.

Catalysts

All of the ideas contained in this book are intended as catalysts—sparks to get our creative juices flowing. When I am playing or composing, it helps having these developmental ideas close at hand, which I can tap into when my musical instincts need some inspiration.

Remember, though: Ideas do not make music, people do. Keep this in mind, as you continue with the Pitch Motif Studies, and the other exercises in this book.

More Pitch Motif Studies

Before moving onto 3-note motifs, let's try one more single-interval study. Working the thirds in "Eh-Tood-Ah with Spice" inspired a calypso-like rhythm, hence the "sambalypso" feel. Now, let's see what an interval of a *fourth* can produce.

To compose this next tune, I began by sketching in the first three bars using fourths in a general ascending line. I then felt inspired to "answer" and contrast the first three bars by using the interval of a seventh through bars 4, 5, and 6 with a general descending line. This seemed like a good beginning for a medium-fast modal swing tune. *Modal* means that a harmonic progression stays in one scale (mode) for an extended time. In the solo section of this tune, two different modes are used in the progression. The D *Dorian* mode (C major scale starting on the second degree) is used for four bars, then four bars of E-flat *Lydian* mode (B-flat major scale starting on the fourth degree). (Mode sheets, for your reference, can be found in Foundations, chapter 6.)

Let's try this melody together, and then you can solo on the modal progression. Solo for thirty-two bars, which is the written solo progression four times through. Then return to the melody, as written, for the ending. On your solo, try to use fourths and sevenths, continuing the interval motifs used in the melody. If you wish, play the melody and solo rhythmically in DrumMode first (see chapter 1) until you are comfortable with the pitches and the form.

D Minor Tune

Fig. 2.6. D Minor Tune

The 3-Note Motif

I am fortunate to have had a wonderful composition teacher, Jeronimas Kacinskas. My most vivid memory of him is the day I excitedly brought in the score for a 10-minute orchestral piece, which Mr. Kacinskas had assigned to me. I was confident in the brilliance of my composition. After several moments of leafing through the score, Mr. Kacinskas turned to page 8, pointed to a bar of music, and asked in his cool Lithuanian accent, "Where did this idea come from?"

After some stammering, I confessed that I couldn't trace the evolution of this bar of music. My confidence was shaken. Mr. Kacinskas then moved to the first page of the score, pointed to a bar of music and asked. "Where did this bar of music go to?"

The realization struck that I wasn't holding a composition in my hands. I was holding a string of technical ideas that were unconnected. No evolution. Mr. Kacinskas said, "You are working too hard. Take advantage of an idea you have and work with it. Don't throw it away and grab another. This is inefficient writing." I also began to realize that my playing improvisation had a similar dilemma. Endless technical ideas (licks). No evolution.

So, I decided to search for a musical idea that would be small enough to be flexible, but big enough to have enough musical personality to be a hook— something that grabs attention, and was recognizable and developable. My search ended with the 3-note melodic motif. It is small enough to be flexible, and, as you will see when you take this musical Rorschach test, powerful.

The Musical Rorschach Test (Inkblots)

Fig. 2.7. Inkblot

Hermann Rorschach was a Swiss psychiatrist (shrink) who developed the Rorschach test. The test consisted of ten cards with abstract inkblot designs, which were shown one at a time to patients who would "interpret" the cards with their initial reaction. These ten interpretations were used to evaluate the patient's emotional and intellectual functioning. For example, if the patient responded with "Pizza!!" for six out of the ten cards, than that patient was probably me. I *love* pizza!

So, here is a musical Rorschach test for you. There are ten 3-note motifs—no rhythms, only noteheads. Listen to them on track 15 of the CD. What is your initial reaction? As with the Rorschach test, everyone reacts differently. Each musical motif can be interpreted in several ways. Do any tunes come to mind? The beginnings, the ends, or the middles of tunes? Strong connections can be made, and there is room for evolution. What do you *first* think of? I use this only to illustrate the power and potential of a 3-note melodic motif.

Please send me your ten *initial* reactions! Thanks.

The Musical Rorschach Test (Interval Blots)

Listen to each "blot." What is your first tune reaction? You have five seconds for each!

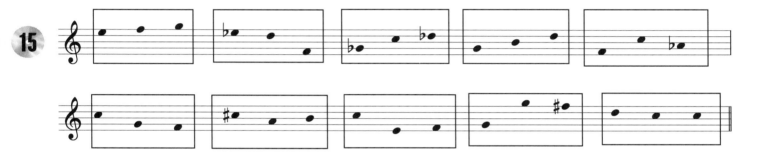

Fig. 2.8. Musical Rorschach Test

Here are some of the benefits you'll gain by observing and using 3-note motifs.

- 3-note motifs are great sparks for your improvisation.

- The 3-note motif is a great melodic building block for composing and improvising because of its physical flexibility. It can be used backwards, upside down, bent in the middle, and so on.

- 3-note motifs make great hooks.

- 3-note motifs are easy to remember.

- Improvising from 3-note motifs found in a tune's melody enables the solo to truly be theme and variation.

- 3-note motifs are strong ear references when accompanying a soloist.

The Palette Chart for Single-Note Development

There are many 3-note melodic motif possibilities. Add rhythmic motif to this and the possibilities are endless. I needed to have an organized plan to work with 3-note motifs, so I came up with the Palette Chart (fig. 2.10), which is simply a chart of 3-note possibilities. In this chapter, we will explore the chart to find melodic material. In chapter four, we will explore the chart for 3-note chordal or harmonic material.

Palette Chart "Seeds" Orientation

Here is how it works. Each two-number group represents the two consecutive intervals that make up a 3-note motif. The first number is the interval between the first and second notes of the motif, and the second number is the interval between the second and third notes. The intervals are diatonic (in the key) of the scale you are using. For starters, let's look how the numbers work, using a good old C major scale. I refer to each number group as a *seed* because, after a while, they start to sprout some pretty cool ideas!

Numbers represent the intervals of 3-note motifs. Here are some seeds from a C major scale:

Here are some seeds from an A major scale:

Here are some seeds from an E melodic minor scale:

Fig. 2.9. Seeds Orientation

The Palette Chart

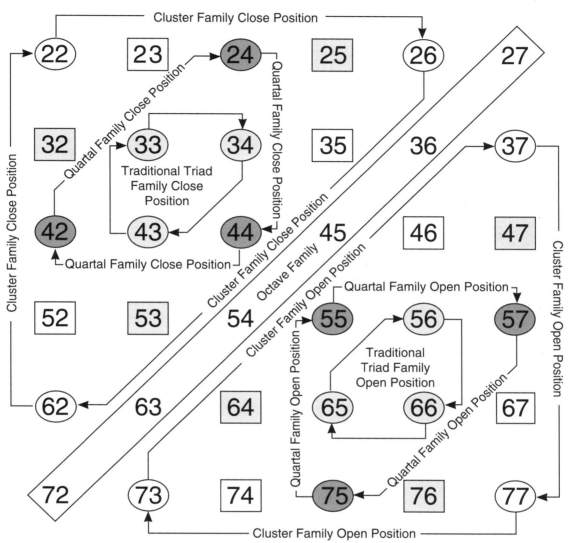

Fig. 2.10. The Palette Chart

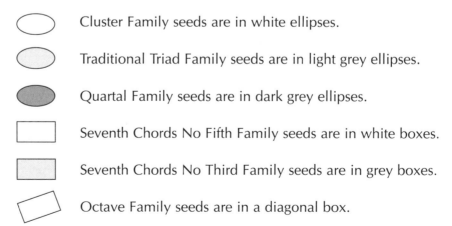

Cluster Family seeds are in white ellipses.

Traditional Triad Family seeds are in light grey ellipses.

Quartal Family seeds are in dark grey ellipses.

Seventh Chords No Fifth Family seeds are in white boxes.

Seventh Chords No Third Family seeds are in grey boxes.

Octave Family seeds are in a diagonal box.

A good way to study these motifs is by carrying them through an entire scale. Play these next exercises over a simple vamp; you can use "Vamp No. 2," (track 11), or the upcoming "Vamp No. 3," (track 16). Work these along the strings. They will be easier to visualize. The numbers represent the 3-note motifs' intervals.

Palette Chart Seeds

Through a C Major Scale

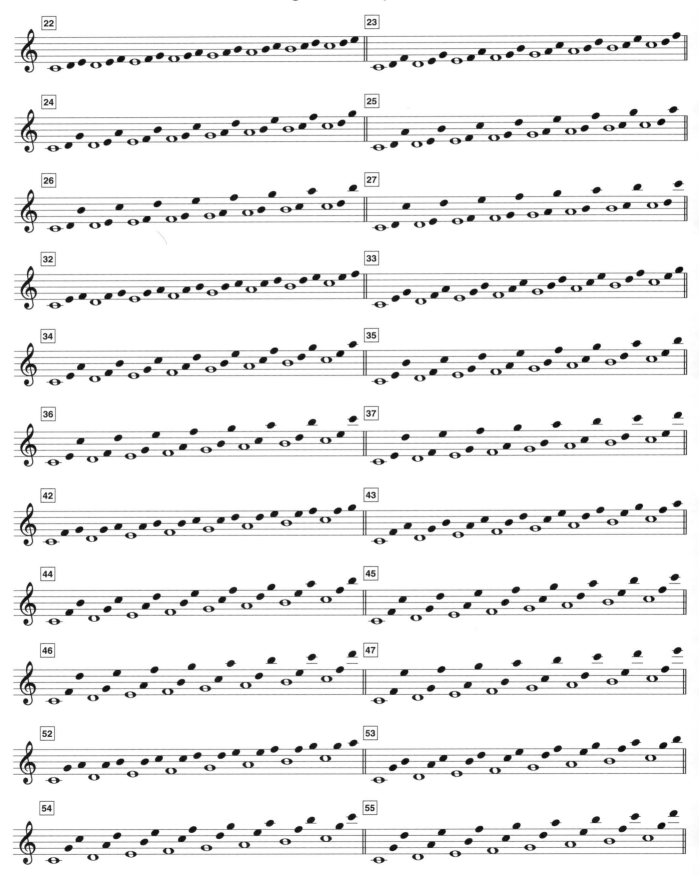

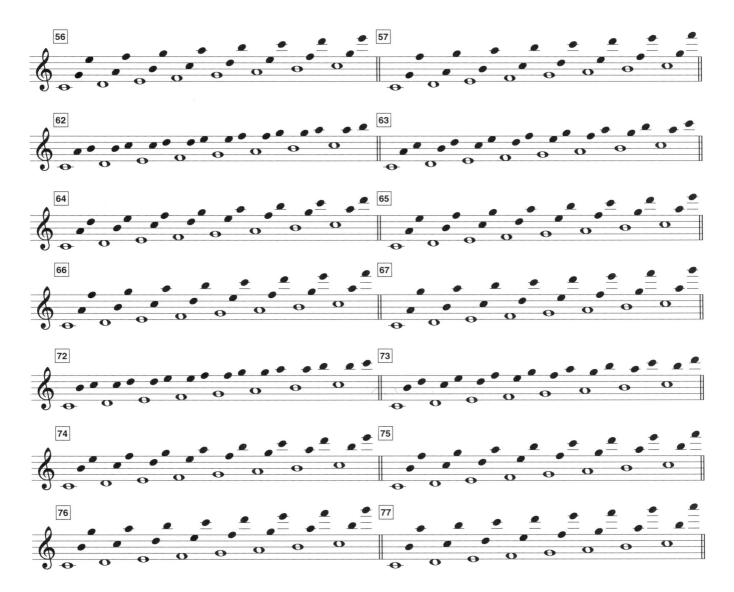

Fig. 2.11. Palette Chart "Seeds"
through the C Major Scale

The preceding exercises are simply scale studies, but instead of just running up and down a scale, you are moving developmentally with a motif. This will build your ability to remember the "character" of an idea, which will help you develop it. For fingerboard templates illustrating these 3-note structures, and other study materials, refer to chapters 4 and 6. They will help you find these 3-note ideas on the guitar.

Play the Palette Chart melodic "seeds" over this vamp.

Vamp No. 3

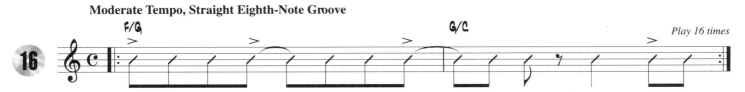

Fig. 2.12. Vamp No. 3

| CAUTION! | CAUTION! | CAUTION! | CAUTION! |

When you see this warning, *DO NOT PANIC!* It is simply a warning that the intellectual ideas presented are *not* music, unless *you* make them music by playing them *musically*. Don't just look at them! Play them over the vamps. Let them inspire you to write something. Get the ideas into your musical belly by singing them. This is much like eating them, since when you sing a musical idea, it is absorbed (digested) into a deeper understanding of that idea. Remember, you play what you eat!

"With the addition of a third note, a simple phenomenon occurs: the potential for contrast or creation of a hook."

—Albert Einstein

(only kidding, it's me!)

Hook and Variations

Hook   A length of metal, bent to point in the opposite direction in order to catch something.

Let's make some real hooks out of the "original" motifs by bending them in the following ways. First, we will change the order of the notes.

Change of Order Variations

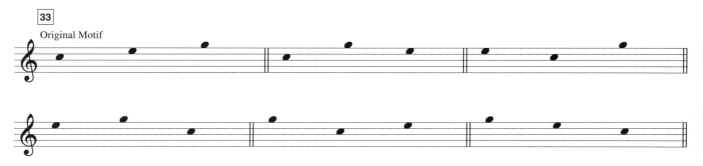

Fig. 2.13. Change of Order Variations

Next are some variations created by changing the octave of some of the motif's notes. This is called *octave adjustment*.

Change of Octave Variations

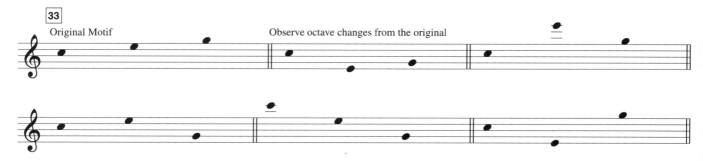

Fig. 2.14. Change of Octave Variations

Here is a light funky tune that starts with a 3-note 53 motif, put through some octave and order variations. The same original notes are used throughout this example—just with octave and order variations. As before, the limitations can lead to unlimited possibilities! I labeled and boxed the original and the first two variations; you can label the rest. For a challenge, try composing an example using only three notes, their octaves, and order variations. You can make your etudes anything they want to be.

Hook Etude in C
Change of Order and Octave Variations

Fig. 2.15. Hook Etude

We'll do just one more Pitch Motif Study before moving onward. In this next study, I used a variation of a jazz standard's opening motif, which is why this study is called "Variations on a Sunny Tune." (Can you guess the jazz standard?) I used the motif to build a solo on the tune (it could even be its own tune). The original's motif, which is used throughout the original melody, is a 23 motif. I put it through some change-of-order variations. This example shows how using the original melodic material of a tune in your improvisation or development section is, as Jeronimas Kacinskas would say (again, with that thick Lithuanian accent), "efficient composing."

Variations on a Sunny Tune
With 23 Motif

Fig. 2.16. Variations on a Sunny Tune

Notice the chromatic approach notes I use to "jazz" things up: the F-sharp to the G in bar 1, the A-flat to G in bar 3, the G-flat to F in bar 4, and the F-sharp to G in the last bar.

Some Simple Language!

In the previous pages, specific interval descriptions (e.g., 26 and 46) were used to delineate 3-note ideas, in order to continue their development. Now, let's use more simple language. Words like "little," "big," and "bigger" will be used instead. Rather than "26" to describe the two intervals of a 3-note motif in "original" form, let's use "up little, up bigger" as the description. With this more basic description of the 3-note idea, our development or "repetitions" of the original motif will be more subtle, and possibly more interesting. Since *little* and *bigger* are relative terms, "26" and "34" both fit this description! And so do "47" and "37." Wow! So, the interpretation of "little" and "bigger" will be up to *you*!

You may ask, "Jon, why didn't you start with simple language description *then* move onto specific details like intervals?" Here is the reason, which can be boring to read so I am putting it in smaller type.

The Reason: First of all, it's the guitar's fault. The way the guitar is built, sometimes "going up" is actually "going down" when moving across the strings (from one edge of the fingerboard to the other). To move a note up *along* a single string, our fingers move away from the pegboard. To move down a note, our fingers move towards the pegboard. But when moving *across the strings*, we can move *up* to a higher pitched note on a another string, but our fingers move *towards the pegboard*. So, simple language can be confusing relative to the guitar until you understand this confusion. Sorry for this boring stuff. I kinda wish the guitar had only one string! Again, it's the guitar's fault!

Now that you have done the interval studies, you know up from down, so let's try some improvisation together, describing our ideas using simple language.

19   **Simple Language Improv No. 1**

In this first improvisation, in the key of G major, I will start with a 3-note *small-bigger* motif with direction variations. Then I will play other motifs. Describe these motifs to yourself in basic language. It is a nice way to observe the other players in an ensemble. You can play ideas that are similar to these motifs, or do anything you want!

I will start playing 3-note motifs *small, bigger,* sometimes *up,* and sometimes *down.* Then, we'll try other motifs. Let's observe them with simple language and use simple language to build our improvisations. We'll close with the *small-bigger* motifs. Let's interchange, baby!

20   **Simple Language Improv No. 2**

Let's try another improvisation together, but this time, we'll *play more freely, keywise.* Let's begin playing 3-note *small-bigger* motifs as before, sometimes up and sometimes down. Then try other motifs—anything goes! As before, observe them with simple language and use simple language to build your improvisations. Then close with *small-bigger* motifs. Let's interchange freely this time!

We are almost ready to close up our work with 3-note melodic motifs, for now. It actually is an endless topic. Before moving onto compound lines, here are a few more ideas.

The "Rebound" Effect in Melodic Construction

Let's expand the "hook" concept into longer melodic ideas.

The word "contrast" is used in this book for good reason. As mentioned earlier, repetition and contrast is a key to keeping an energy level in any artistic endeavor, from architecture to painting.

It is found here in the *rebound effect.* A general direction tendency in melodic construction is to move with small intervals in one direction and then rebound by leaping a larger interval in the other direction. Also, a leap in one direction may be followed by small intervals in the other direction. The series of smaller intervals creates a tightening effect, which is released by the interval leap in the opposite direction. You can observe this tendency in single-note lines, from Mozart to bebop.

This next tune, "Poiple," is a clear example of rebound effect. It is a simple ballad from *Apple Stew*, a suite composed for my hometown New York, the Big Apple.

Poiple

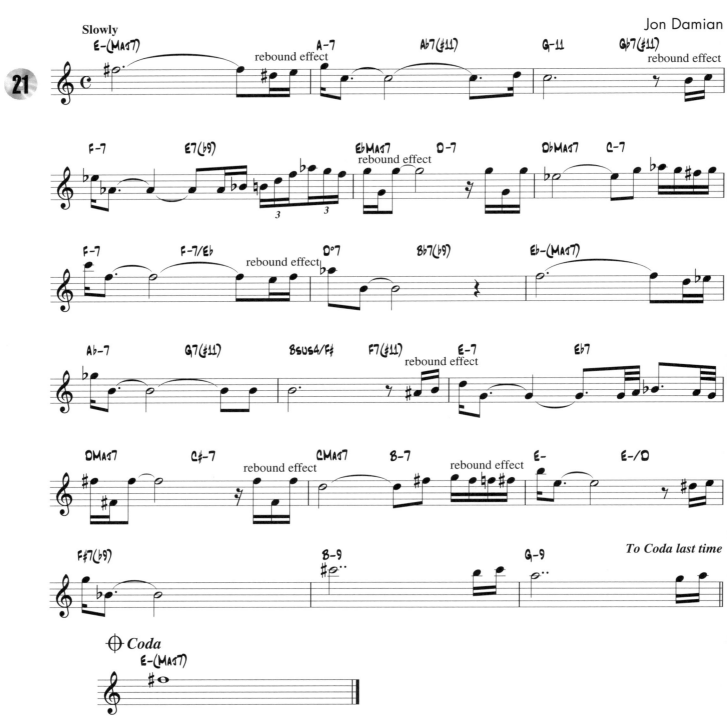

Fig. 2.17. Poiple

Octave Adjustment

Octave adjustment is a powerful technique that can add variety to melodic ideas. I have always been jealous of saxophone players, who have an octave key (operated by their thumb) that changes a note's octave. So, on the saxophone, a particular melody can be put through some nice variations with the octave key. On the guitar, playing the octave of a note takes a bit more work, but is very effective.

First, try taking a simple scale and changing some of its notes to other octaves. Here is an example.

G Major Scale with Octave Adjustment
Lines indicate octave change (adjustment)

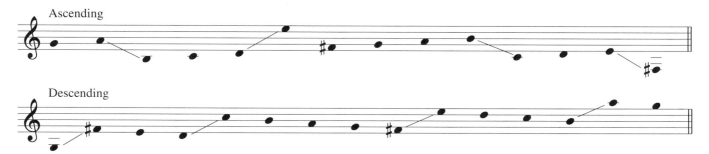

Fig. 2.18. Scale with Octave Adjustment

In "Rondo a la Ralph," written for my buddy Ralph, the theme was created using octave adjustment. The *foundation* (basic melody before octave adjustment) is simply arpeggiated chords (see bottom staff). I changed the octaves of some notes to create the first eight bars. By using octave adjustment, instead of continually jumping by thirds, wider leaps of sixths and tenths are produced. This creates a *compound line*—the melody has two or more melodies within it. Compound lines will be discussed in detail later in this chapter.

Rondo a la Ralph

Fig. 2.19. Rondo a la Ralph

Quodlibet (pronounced "quode lee-bay")

Here is a nice pick-pocketing technique called *quodlibet.* Sounds like a Canadian hockey player, doesn't it? Actually it's a melodic rip-off technique. It simply means taking a commonly known melodic idea and using it (quoting it) in an improvisation or composition. The saxophonist Dexter Gordon and the composer Charles Ives are well noted for using this technique in their work. It is a powerful technique when used well and an obnoxious one when not. As I am writing this, it happens to be Christmas season, and it seems that on every Christmas party gig somebody has to quote "Jingle Bells" in their solo. This is a case of obnoxious use, but it's still fun. Lately I have been quoting the opening line of George Gershwin's "It Ain't Necessarily So" in solos, and it's a cool melodic idea.

Here is an excerpt from a composition called "Bye-Bop," in which I use bits and pieces of two *common* bebop tunes and weave them together. Can you guess the tunes? Use your eyes and ears. The answers are in Foundations (chapter 6), on the Crossword Puzzle page, if you need to peek. This is a purely melodic tune, since there are no chord changes. It is filled with lots of juicy 3-note motifs you can use in your solos.

Can you guess the two bebop tunes?

Bye-Bop
An Excerpt

Jon Damian

Fig. 2.20. Bye-Bop

Extended composition continues...

Compound Lines

Before moving on to chapter 3, Counterpoint, let's explore one more concept of melodic construction and development: compound lines. A single-note melodic line can be simple or compound. A simple single-note melodic line consists of one simple line, which could be built using perhaps a repeated note, stepwise melodic direction, or an arpeggio. A *compound line* is a single-note line that "brings together" *two or more* simple lines. A compound line is still monophonic (one note at a time), but the line has an interaction—a counterpoint between the simple lines that comprise it.

Here is an example of a simple melody—a bit of "What A Perfect Love," written for Ralph's wedding. The melody moves essentially by step, with an occasional leap.

What a Perfect Love
To Terry and Ralph

Jon Damian

Fig. 2.21. "What a Perfect Love." An example of a single melodic line.

Second A section continues...

The Three Compound Lines in Simple Language

Two elements moving at the same time—dancers, acrobats, soccer players, and in this case, simple melodies—can move in the *same direction* together. This is called *similar direction*. There are two possibilities: *together up* and *together down*.

Here is an example of a *similar direction* compound line from J.S. Bach's *Partita No. 1 for Solo Violin*. In this melody, there are *three* simple melodies moving in similar motion. Observe how Bach articulates each of these three lines differently, using bow markings (slurs). This further distinguishes each line.

Articulations (bow markings) indicate each line of the compound line.

Partita No. 1 for Solo Violin

Fig. 2.22. An excerpt from Partita No. 1 for Solo Violin, *by J.S.Bach.*
An example of a similar-direction compound line.

One simple melody can *repeat* a single note or melodic figure while the other simple melody moves towards or away from the repeated idea. This is called *oblique direction*. There are five possibilities with oblique direction:

1. Upper line repeats, bottom line moves upward.

2. Upper line repeats, bottom line moves downward.

3. Lower line repeats, upper line moves upward.

4. Lower line repeats, upper line moves downward.

5. One line repeats, other line moves above and below.

Here is an example of (5), from J.S. Bach's *The Well-Tempered Clavier*.

Notehead shapes indicate each line of a compound line.

Excerpt from *The Well-Tempered Clavier*

Fig. 2.23. An excerpt from The Well-Tempered Clavier *by J. S. Bach.*
An example of an oblique-direction compound line.

For another look at an oblique-direction compound line in action, here is an excerpt from a Jim Hall solo on his composition "Romaine," from the wonderful recording with Bill Evans, *Undercurrents.* Observe the return to the B-flat note, as indicated.

Romaine

Note the repeating B♭ as the returning point for the oblique direction.

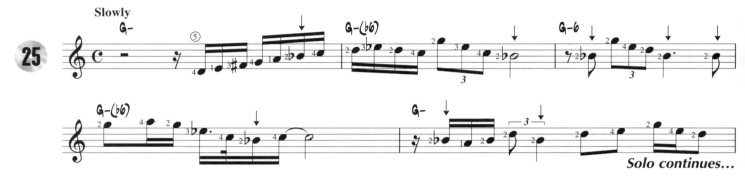

Fig. 2.24. An excerpt from a Jim Hall solo on his composition "Romaine."
Another example of an oblique direction compound line.

When the two simple melodies move *towards* each other or *away from* each other, the motion is called *contrary motion.* There are two possibilities with contrary motion: moving towards each other or moving away from each other.

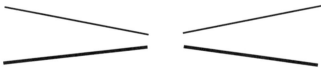

Here is a contrary direction example—an excerpt from "Clicheicity," a blues head we'll look at more closely later.

Clicheicity

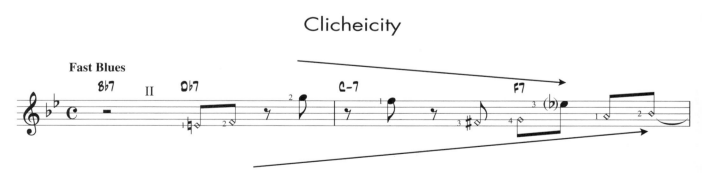

Fig. 2.25. An exerpt from "Clicheicity," an example of a contrary direction compound line. Notehead shapes indicate each voice of compound line.

How and Where to Begin?

So, how and where should you begin incorporating compound lines into your improvisational and compositional vocabulary? Begin with your ears, and observe the single-note lines all around you. Imagine the lines visually. Is it a simple or a compound line? Make musical sketches (think of them as doodles). Observing new ideas with pencil and paper will help you use the ideas on your instrument.

Here are some guitar-friendly ideas to help you incorporate compound lines into your improvisational technique.

The Oblique-Direction Compound Line in Action

The guitar is well designed for compound-line improvisation. Let's begin with the easiest compound line: oblique direction. Since one line isn't moving, there is less "to keep track of." In similar and contrary direction compound lines, both lines are moving.

Start on the G string. Use the open G for the repeating line, and on the fingerboard for the moving line. The open string will be easy to find, when needed. You'll improvise on a G blues, using oblique direction.

Let's start things off together with a melody on the G string. Then *you* improvise on only the G string for two choruses, and then we'll finish with the melody. This tune is called "Oblique Blues."

Oblique Blues
A tune and improvisation on the G string

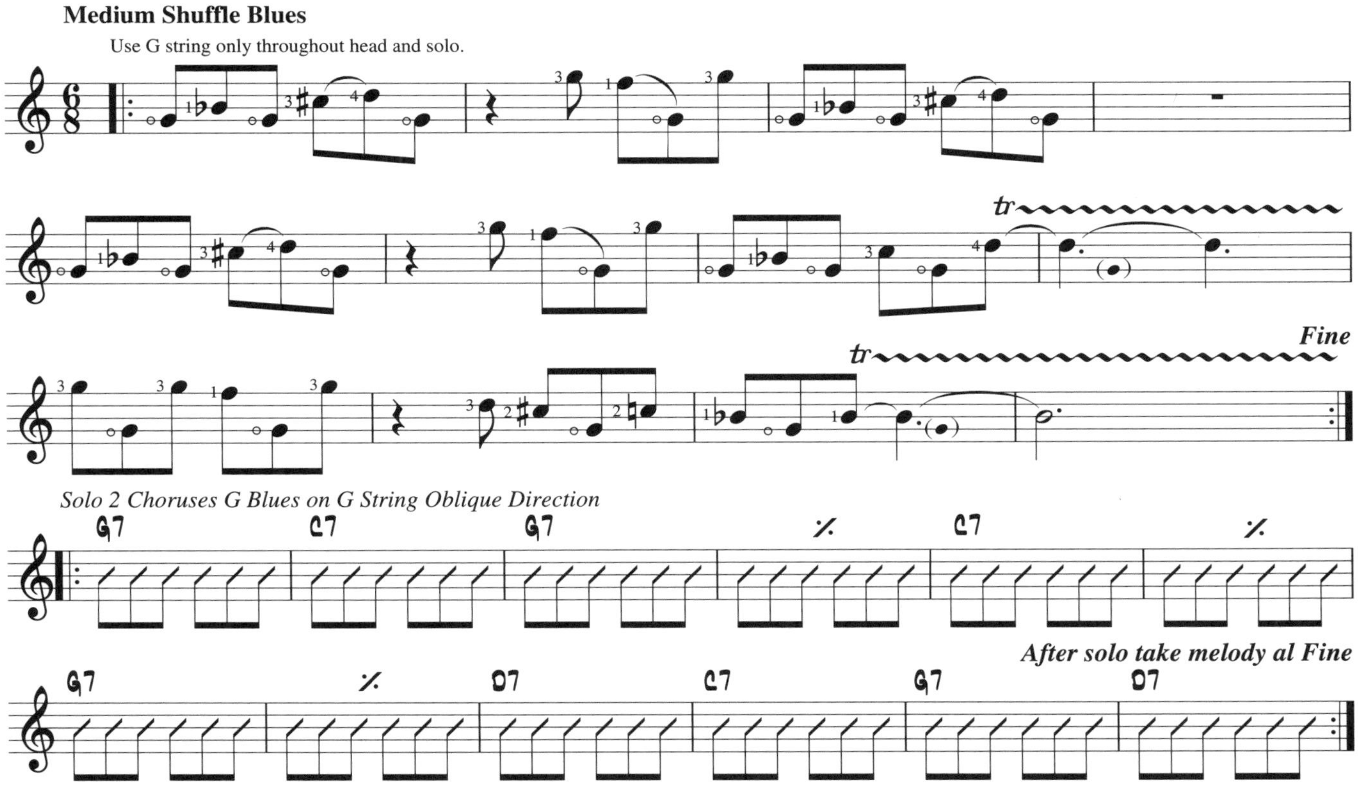

Fig. 2.26. Oblique Blues

Another guitar-friendly idea for oblique direction is using an open string as part of a regular chord progression. Here are two examples.

27

An oblique idea using one-chord fingering and the open G string

Here is a variety of voicings with oblique direction.

Fig. 2.27. Oblique Direction Examples

More detailed oblique studies will be introduced a bit later. First, we'll explore similar direction.

The Similar-Direction Compound Line in Action

Let's use that G blues track again (track 26), but this time, use only the B and D strings for your improvisation. Because of the automatic interval separation between the B and D strings, compound lines will result. Moving *along* the two strings in one direction produces similar direction. As we learned from Samisen Sam (chapter 1), using a limited area of the instrument really opens up new possibilities.

The Contrary-Direction Compound Line in Action

Contrary direction is the most difficult compound line to incorporate, but one of the most dramatic, as we saw in the Direction section of chapter 1. Try staying on only one string at first. This will help you to visualize the two contrary moving lines. Then try moving with two strings. Play a bit *up* one of the strings, then answer by playing a bit *down* the other string.

Some Compound-Line Scale Patterns

Let's take a more detailed look at how to incorporate the compound line into your playing. Here is a series of compound-line patterns built on various scales. Complete the pattern through the rest of the scale; only the patterns on the first two scale degrees are shown. One line of the compound line is notated with regular noteheads; the other has diamond shapes.

This series is only scratching the surface of possibilities. Transfer these patterns to a variety of scale types. Let each pattern inspire an improvisation. *See* the music within these ideas. Imagine yourself "doodling" with the various shapes of single-note lines.

Discover your own patterns; the possibilities are endless.

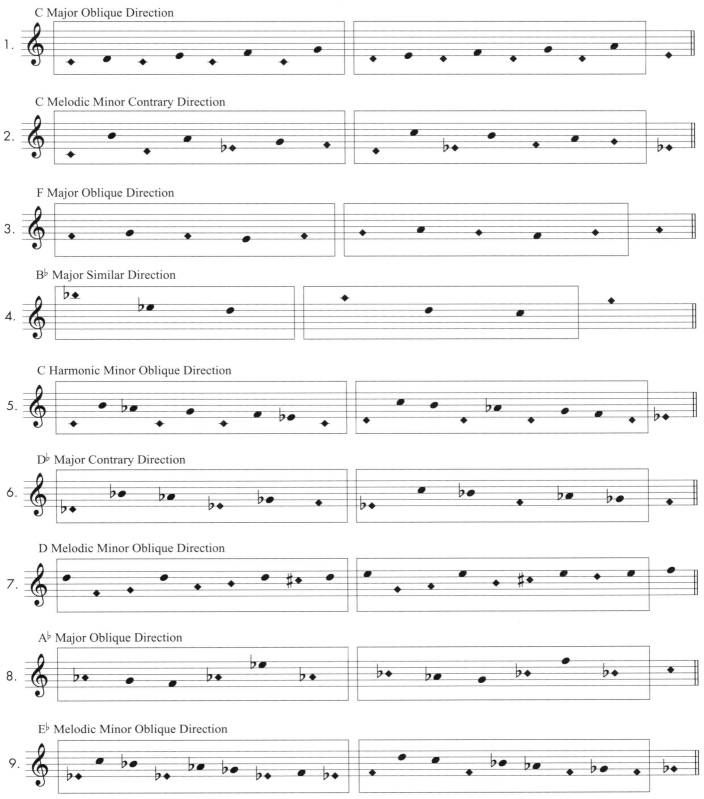

Fig. 2.28. Compound-Line Scale Patterns

"Clicheicity" is a B-flat blues etude that incorporates all the compound lines. The lines are distinguished by different noteheads.

Clicheicity

Fig. 2.29. Clicheicity

The concept of compound lines is linear. As you will see, this is good preparation to study counterpoint, where you will follow the development of two ideas moving in a particular direction relationship (similar, oblique, or contrary) to one another. Incorporating this concept as a creative melodic resource takes some work, but eventually it will become a part of your musical instinct. In fact, compound lines are more natural in concept than are many nonlinear melodic ideas. Of course, in certain improvisational situations, there is a harmonic progression to respect. But attention to the harmony should never interfere with the linear integrity of the melodic ideas.

Transcription

The concepts included in this chapter are designed to build your melodic curiosity and develop your independent thinking about creating your own melodies. Part of exploring melodic possibilities is studying the melodic masters through *transcription*—using your ears and writing down the solos of the master improvisers and the compositions (tunes) of the master composers.

Art students do the same thing, visiting museums to copy (transcribe) paintings by master artists. I once asked the wonderful painter Jane Goldman why she directed her students to "transcribe" the masters' works. She replied, "It's like a musician figuring out a horn line. If you can break it down and figure out how they did it, you achieve an understanding of what was played. The sum is greater than the parts."

In Closing

Studying the world of single-note melodic ideas is endless, and it could easily fill volumes. I hope this humble chapter inspires your own distinctive melodic world. We will explore more single-note ideas in Counterpoint (chapter 3) and The Palette Chart (chapter 4). Let's close up this party with one final compound line: an oblique-direction idea.

You can use just your G string for this, if you like.

Fig. 2.30. Compound-Line Oblique Direction Idea

Thanks again for celebrating with me!

Chapter 3 Counterpoint

"The journey is the reward."

—Chinese Proverb

For some reason, the word "counterpoint" has a really neat sound to it. "Oh Charles, did you hear the intriguing counterpoint between the second violin and viola in the fifth Bartók quartet?" It's an impressive word because counterpoint is impressive sounding stuff. But what exactly is it?

Counterpoint is all around us! It is the interaction between two or more things. The rhythm of our walking interacting with the pulse of our heartbeats. The interaction in our conversations. Two dancers on a stage. Any simultaneous occurrence of two or more activities creates counterpoint. Even the components of a car engine. Of course, getting these interacting activities to also *work* together in a cohesive way is another matter—and expensive, if you use the same auto mechanic I do!

Let's look at a definition of "counterpoint" from a musical perspective:

Counterpoint   The combination of two or more musical ideas in a working relationship, while maintaining the individuality of each idea.

The guitar is a great tool to study counterpoint. Counterpoint sounds great on the guitar. A 2-line counterpoint can "sound bigger" than 4-, 5-, or 6-note chords, because the distinct tone colors of each line can be distinguished more clearly with only two lines. With six strings or voices on the guitar, there are a lot of color possibilities.

The following counterpoint studies are offered simply to create a departure point or *catalyst* for your own ideas, as discussed in chapter 2. It is up to you to hop on and make the music, and to create the breath of musical life, using the basic sound dimensions (see chapter 1). The studies will build your ability to be in two places at the same time. As mentioned, counterpoint is the interaction of two or more things. Let's try an improvisation on our guitar using two simple elements—two strings.

Some Simple Canons

Most counterpoint books don't introduce canons until about a third of the way through a three-hundred page book, but since they sound so cool, I'd like to start with some. In fact, we already tried some direction canons together in *The Coronation* (chapter 1).

In a canon, the melody (single-note idea) in one voice is repeated a bit later in another voice, while the first voice continues. "Row, Row, Row Your Boat" and "Three Blind Mice" are classic examples of simple canons that you've probably sung before. This repetition in other voices creates a strong diagonal structure. And it sounds nice, too.

Canon Variations

Canon Variation No. 1

This first contrapuntal study (sounds cool already) will use two simple elements on the guitar: the low E string (bottom string) and the high E string (top string). You can decide which notes to play. If you want to stay in one scale, that is up to you. If not, that's up to you, also.

First, play any two notes (any frets) on the *high* E string. Play notes from an E major or E minor scale, if you wish. Then play the same two notes (frets) on the *low* E string as an answer (the same notes, two octaves lower). Repeat this pattern in a steady rhythm until it is comfortable. Remember to vary the notes you play, but always answer with the same frets (notes) on the low E string as you did on the high E string. You are playing a simple canon— again, a composition in which the same melody is repeated in another voice or line (in this case, another string), starting at different times. That's what we're doing here!

How Canon Variation No. 1 Might Look and Sound

Use high E string only for top line of canon.

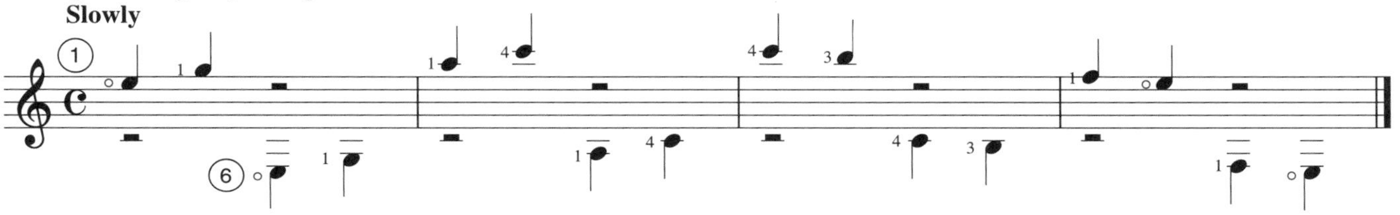

Use low E string only for bottom line of canon.

Fig. 3.1. Canon Variation No. 1

Canon Variation No. 2

Play any two notes (any frets) on the *high* E string, as in variation 1, but play the open *low* E string *at the same time.* Let it ring out for two beats.

Then, play the same two frets on the low E string, and play the open high E string *at the same time.* Let it ring out, as above.

You should be playing two notes on one E string against the other open E string.

Continue the pattern, vary the notes. Take it somewhere.

Variation No. 2 may look something like this.

How Canon Variation No. 2 Might Look and Sound

Use high E string only for top line of canon.

Use low E string only for bottom line of canon.

Fig. 3.2. Canon Variation No. 2

Canon Variation No. 3

Use variations 1 and 2, but play three or four notes before changing voices.

Also, try using different strings.

Take it somewhere.

Variation 3 may look something like this.

How Canon Variation No. 3 Might Look and Sound

Use high E string only for top line of canon.

Use low E string only for bottom line of canon.

Fig. 3.3. Canon Variation No. 3

These canon variations, utilizing the high and low E strings, will get you started with canonic counterpoint (I told you it sounded cool!). Using these two strings is guitar friendly, since both strings are laid out exactly the same, two octaves apart. This makes the canonic "response" easy to visualize since the E strings are reflections of one another.

This is only a beginning. As you create canons in various tonalities and scale types, visualization becomes more of a challenge. Developing an awareness of scales and intervals, and an ability to use octave adjustment (chapter 2), will make this easier.

This awareness of scales, intervals, and octaves will become increasingly important as you explore other aspects of counterpoint. To practice scales, intervals, and octave adjustment, see chapter 6 (particularly the Cycle Scales, Jaws, and Zorro studies).

A Crash Course

This chapter attempts a very simple, general discussion of counterpoint, geared toward guitarists who wish to explore contrapuntal techniques in their improvisation. The more detailed discussions of counterpoint found in the standard texts are also important for study. Techniques such as formal canon and fugue are timeless concepts for the composer. One of my favorite texts (for me, it is the easiest to read) is "The Study of Counterpoint," from *Gradus Ad Parnassum*, by Johann Joseph Fux. The book is in the form of a dialogue between the master Aloysius and the student Josephus, so it flows nicely. But for now, let's keep things simple.

Counterpoint is essentially two musical ideas working together. As you will see, these ideas can be single-note lines or chord structures. For now, our work will be with two single-note lines.

Any two single-note lines occurring simultaneously can be called "counterpoint," and there are many possibilities. But does the counterpoint work? Any two folks can dance simultaneously, but is there an interrelationship of some kind between them? Is there rhythm? A sense of time? Some agreement as to essential body movement? And is there contrast or *surprise* of body movement—for example, contrary direction, with the dancers moving apart and then returning together? In the dance of two single-note lines of counterpoint, these same elements—rhythm and contrast—are just as important. Is there an agreement as to where the time (tempo) is? What tonality (key) and progression (harmonic intent) is desired? Are there elements of surprise and contrast?

Before any surprises, the dancers must be able to move well together so that the audience has a point of reference. Similarly, in music, having two lines of counterpoint in the same key and tempo is the first step in creating a point of reference for contrasts, departures, and returns.

Species-One Counterpoint

In this first series of studies, the two lines of counterpoint will move in the same rhythmic values, in the same key, and with consonant (restful) intervals between the two lines. In official counterpoint language, this is called species-one counterpoint.

Let's start with a study using a simple key center, like C major. The examples move through the C major scale using the restful or consonant intervals of diatonic thirds and sixths only. These intervals will move through the scale by step (in intervals of seconds) and/or leap (anything but an interval of a second). Eventually, you should do this exercise using all scale types and keys. Remember, this is a crash course; the rest is up to you!

CAUTION!   CAUTION!   CAUTION!   CAUTION!

Remember, the intellectual ideas presented are *not* music unless you make them music by playing them *musically.* Don't just look at them! Play them!

Species-One Studies

Play *each* species-one study as written, with rhythmic and dynamic ideas of your choice, until you are comfortable with it. Then move the study to another key or scale quality, for some contrast. Finally, return to the original example. Remember, these studies, with your musical help, are potentially pieces of music. Feel free to use rhythmic, dynamic, and emotional variety, as you wish. Notice in studies 5 and 6 how the intervalic alternation between the third and the sixth creates some interesting direction motion between the two voices.

These studies are simply scale studies seen from another perspective. Add them to your comprovisational resources; they will help you use scales creatively (as will many of the studies in this book). As mentioned before, these species-one studies, using only the intervals of thirds and sixths, are a foundation for further studies. There are more possible variations then these seven possibilities. Find your own.

Species-One Studies

Fig. 3.4. Some Species-One Studies

Remember, you must always be musical when playing these studies. Maintain the highest respect for your musical integrity, and play everything at your highest possible level. Doing less is a bad habit. Also, when your musical imagination is at work, seemingly simple ideas become creative sparks for improvisation and composition development.

Here is a piece, "Species One Samba," a sketch built primarily out of thirds and sixths. By limiting myself to these intervals, I found new possibilities. The piece begins in G melodic minor for four bars, briefly moves up to B-flat melodic minor, then back to G minor by way of A-flat melodic minor. For a color change, G harmonic minor is used for two bars, over a D *pedal* (repeated note), added for support and some oblique direction interest. Chromatic motion is then used for two bars, moving to a G major sound to brighten things up a bit. Chord symbols could be added later.

Let's listen to "Species One Samba," and then play it a couple of times together.

Species One Samba

Fig. 3.5. Species One Samba

It was tempting to put in other intervals besides thirds and sixths in "Species One Samba" for contrast, but I fought off the temptation. I actually like the way the thirds and the sixths create a warmth and a *tonal clarity;* there is little doubt as to whether a sound is major or minor. Later, we will work with counterpoint in which tonality is less of an issue. For now, tonality will serve as a foundation we are setting in place to build the species-two counterpoint studies.

Species-Two Counterpoint

Now, to put those thirds and sixths to work! Here in species two, the two lines of counterpoint will become rhythmically independent. One line will move, and the other line will sustain. In official counterpoint lingo, the sustaining line is called *cantus firmus* (cool sounding, right?) and the moving line is called *cambiata* (sounds like a new model Chevrolet). Thirds and sixths will now be "targets." Let's begin with a sixth, and put it to work.

Fig. 3.6. A Sixth (6)

As we can hear, this is a nice restful sound, and it is this restfulness that is going to help us here. We'll call the bottom note, the G-natural, the *cantus firmus* (sustained note), and the top note, the E-natural, part of the *cambiata* (changing notes).

Next, let's "pull up" that E-natural a bit to an F-natural, then "drop it back" into place. This creates a simple movement from unrest to rest—a seventh moving to a sixth (F to E, against the cantus G). Since the key is C major, F-natural was used as part of the cambiata. If it was G major, we would have used F-sharp instead.

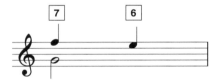

Fig. 3.7. 7 to 6 Above

Now, let's pull down the E-natural a bit to a D-natural, and then let it snap back up.

This is another simple movement—a fifth to a sixth (D to E, against the cantus G).

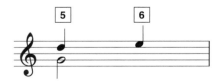

Fig. 3.8. 5 to 6 Above

Let's reverse things. The top note, E-natural, will be the cantus, and the lower note, G-natural, will be part of the cambiata. We'll pull up the G-natural and then let it snap back down—a fifth moving to a sixth.

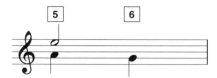

Fig. 3.9. 5 to 6 Below

Then pull the G down to an F, and let it snap back up—a seventh to a sixth.

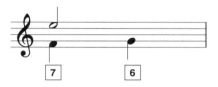

Fig. 3.10. 7 to 6 Below

Now, let's do the same with thirds.

Fig. 3.11. A Third (3)

The bottom note, the C-natural, will be the cantus, and the top note, the E-natural, the cambiata. Pull up that E to an F, then drop it back into place.

This is another simple movement from unrest to rest—a fourth moving to a third.

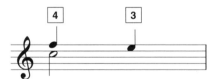

Fig. 3.12. 4 to 3 Above

Pull down the E to a D, and then let it snap back up—a second moving to a third.

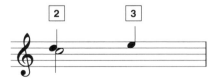

Fig. 3.13. 2 to 3 Above

Again, let's reverse things. The top note E will be the cantus, and the C the cambiata. Pull the C up to a D, and let it snap back down—a second to a third.

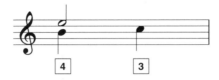

Fig. 3.14. 2 to 3 Below

Pull the C down to a B, and let it snap back up—a fourth to a third.

Fig. 3.15. 4 to 3 Below

Not earth shattering sounds, yet. But, as we will see, in context, these movements can create some really nice counterpoint ideas. You can see why thirds and sixths work nicely as foundations and "targets" for our work.

Before we take some of these counterpoint patterns through some scales, let's look at the various possibilities next to each other for easy reference.

There are four basic possibilities with each interval. Here are the possibilities for sixths: a seventh to a sixth (with the cambiata above or below the cantus) or a fifth to a sixth (again, above or below).

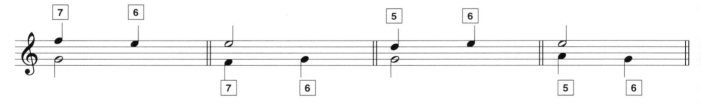

Fig. 3.16. Four Possibilities: Sixths

These are the possibilities for thirds: a fourth to a third (cambiata above or below the cantus) or a second to a third (again, above or below).

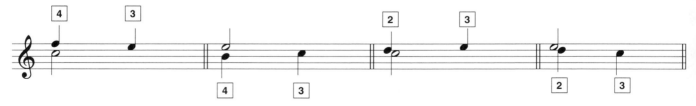

Fig. 3.17. Four Possibilities: Thirds

Think of these possibilities as simple counterpoint cadences.

Now, let's take each of these possibilities through some scales. Each of the following studies will begin a counterpoint pattern. Continue each pattern through the rest of the scale and fingerboard. Write out the rest of the pattern, if you like. Each pattern is labeled. In the first set, the cantus (half notes) moves by step, and the cambiata (quarter notes) moves with it. Some studies use two interval patterns in the cambiata.

Once you have mastered these exercises, make up your own variations of them. You can use other scale types and keys, and begin them on any scale note—not just the tonic or root.

Species-Two Studies

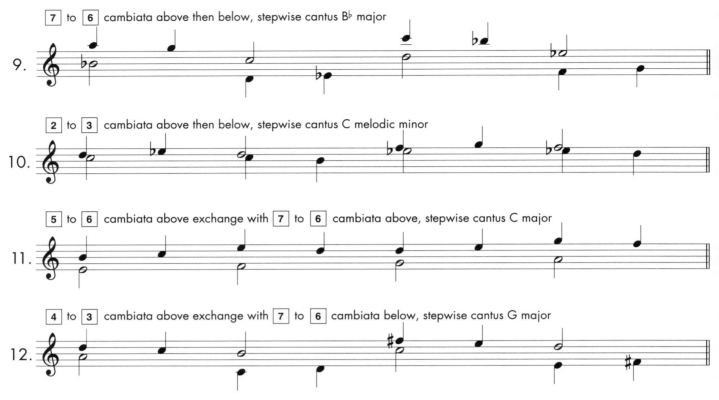

Fig. 3.18. Some Species-Two
Patterns through Scales

The possibilities for using these counterpoint patterns are endless. Find your
own. As you can hear, they are great catalysts for developing contrapuntal
ideas.

Also, try these patterns with rhythmic variation. Here is one pattern with
some possible rhythmic variations:

Fig. 3.19. Species-Two Pattern
with Rhythmic Variation

This next study was created using simple species-two patterns. Notice how
rhythmic variation adds interest throughout the piece. Occasionally, an
ostinato (repeated line) is added to "thicken" up the texture. The piece
moves from A minor to A major. For some reason, as I was sketching this
out, I thought of Bill Leavitt, so the piece is called "For William G." (Bill
Leavitt was chair of Berklee's guitar department for many years and wrote *A
Modern Method for Guitar,* published by Berklee Press).

For William G.
A Species-Two Etude

Jon Damian

Fig. 3.20. For William G.

Here's something a bit different—a funk vamp for two guitars, with some 2-to-3 and 7-to-6 patterns. Let's listen and then play it together.

C7 Funk Vamp with Species Two Patterns

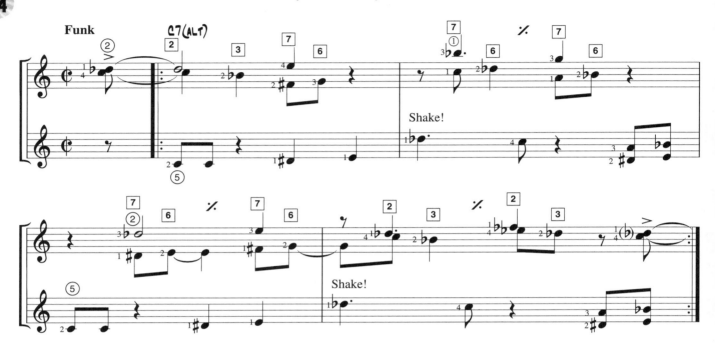

Fig. 3.21. C7 Funk

Two-part counterpoint adds a nice texture to solos and accompaniments. This next example could be a solo or an accompaniment. The two-part counterpoint works as a good transition between the chords. The progression is based on a jazz standard, which is why I call this study "Just Fiends." The scales used as the source for the counterpoint are all labeled. When working with a particular harmonic progression, as in this tune, the counterpoint must respect the chord scales (the tonalities of the chord progression). More about this in Counterpoint from Chord Symbols, later in this chapter, where we set counterpoint to particular chord progressions.

Just Fiends
Etude with Species Two

Fig. 3.22. Just Fiends

The Compound Line as Two-Part Counterpoint

What would the compound-line ideas (chapter 2) sound like if we turned them into two-part counterpoint? Here are a couple of ideas, first in their original "single-note line" form, and then as two-part counterpoint.

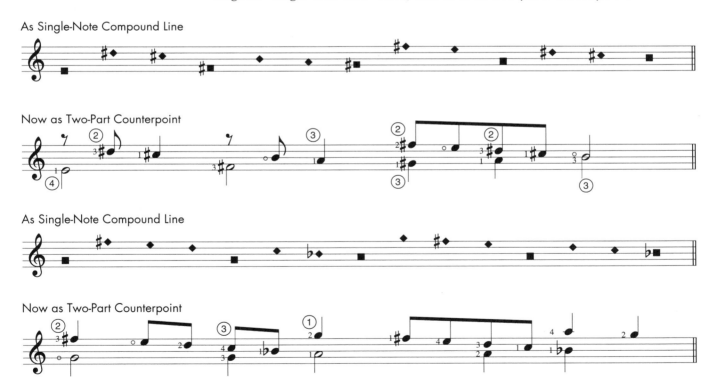

Fig. 3.23. Compound Lines as Two-Part Counterpoint

Two-Part Counterpoint as Single-Note Idea

Next, let's take some of the species-two patterns and make them single-note lines.

They are shown first as counterpoint patterns, and then interpreted as single-note lines.

Counterpoint as a Single-Note Line

Fig. 3.24. Counterpoint as a
Single-Note Line

Counterpoint from Chord Symbols

In this section, we'll use two-part counterpoint within chord progressions—the harmonic form of a composition. With the help of some simple counterpoint "formulas," the counterpoint produced will portray the progressions without actual chords. This is a useful improvisational resource, since the two-part-counterpoint texture is a good contrast to the chord sounds used traditionally.

Use the formulas as guides for study purposes. In these formulas, the numbers refer to the chord-scale degrees of the chord symbol. (For your reference, Vamp Study [chapter 6] shows a series of chord progressions and their relative chord scales.)

Here is a sample formula, illustrated using a Cmaj7 chord symbol. The chord scale is C major.

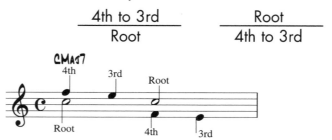

Fig. 3.25. 4th to 3rd over Root

Notice that the counterpoint looks very much like the counterpoint we studied earlier in the chapter. Now, however, the counterpoint is referring to a chord symbol. Observe how the root and the third degree are present here, and in many of the formulas presented here. The third is important because it determines the basic major or minor quality of the chord progression, at that point. In some formulas, there is no third degree present. These chord qualities will be subtler. In formulas with no root, add the root in a third voice to hear the counterpoint color.

Each of the following formulas is demonstrated in an accompanying example. Some of the progressions may look familiar. In these written examples, the scale degrees can occur in any octave. Again, these formulas are only presented here as guides for study. Try these exercises with the formulas, and if you like, write them out.

1. Play through all the examples below.

2. Take *one formula* and carry it through an entire chord progression.

3. Try mixing two or more formulas through a chord progression.

Numbers refer to degrees of chord scales.

Counterpoint from Chord Symbols Formulas

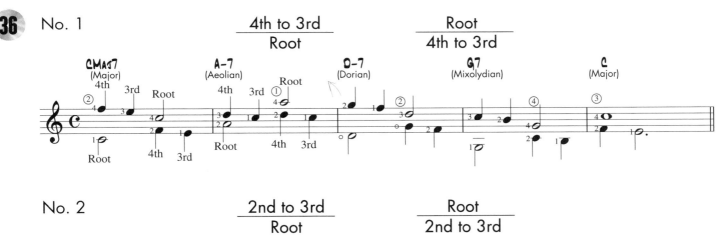

No. 3

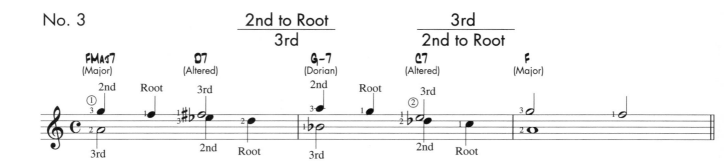

No. 4

No. 5

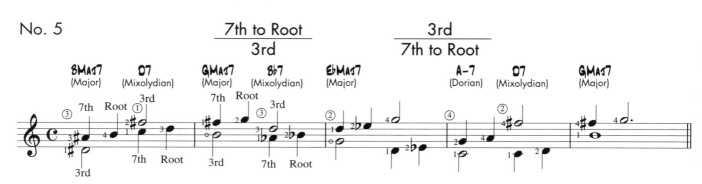

Fig. 3.26. Counterpoint-from-Chord-Symbol Formulas

Here are two more examples that include tension notes in the counterpoint formula. Notice that the intervals of thirds and sixths are still being used as resolutions.

No. 6

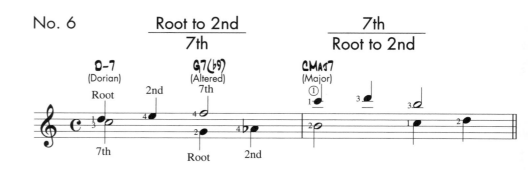

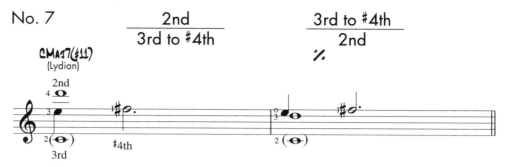

Fig. 3.27. Counterpoint from Chord Symbol Formulas

Here is a 16-bar study using a variety of formulas. I labeled the first two bars. You can label the rest. In bars 7 and 8, notice the 7-to-6 and 2-to-3 counterpoint patterns. In bar 9, rhythmic variations are introduced. The progression may look familiar. That is why this etude is called "All The Things You Thought You Were But Wasn't."

All The Things You Thought You Were But Wasn't
A study using counterpoint from chord-symbol formulas

Fig. 3.28. All The Things You
Thought You Were But Wasn't

Double Combo Special

Here is a simple way to begin to transition these counterpoint ideas into your playing. We will also use this technique in The Palette Chart (chapter 4) and in Form (chapter 5). It is called Double Combo Special, and has nothing to do with Burger King or McDonald's. All you do is combine (combo) a new technique, such as these counterpoint ideas, with a technique you are already comfortable with (such as using standard chord forms). It is sort of like having training wheels when you learn to ride a bicycle.

Here are the first nine bars of "All The Things You Thought You Were But Wasn't," except standard chord forms are used at the beginning of each bar. Complete the rest of the tune using Double Combo Special.

All The Things You Thought You Were But Wasn't
With Double Combo Special

Fig. 3.29. "All The Things You Thought You Were But Wasn't" with Double Combo Special

The Counterpoint Diary

The preceding studies are just the tip of the "contrapuntal iceberg" the guitar has to offer. So far, we have only looked at counterpoint joining two single-note lines that are both in the same key. Since an important goal of this book is to stimulate our compositional senses, I pose a question: What if we wrote counterpoint with two single-note lines but each line was in a different scale? Or made one of the "lines" chords? Or had two tunes at the same time? Or…? My imagination can think of lots of possibilities, and I am sure that yours can too. What I do, since many of my ideas are too involved for me to do right away, is keep a diary of the ideas. I call it my *counterpoint diary.*

Dear Counterpoint Diary,

Here are some excerpts from my counterpoint diary. The diary is filled with sketches of counterpoint ideas that I was curious about. Each diary example is preceded by a verbal description of the idea. There is a description of each layer of counterpoint: the direction between the lines (similar, oblique, or contrary) and their starting interval. Finally, there is the rhythmic ratio between layers.

For example, in my first diary example, the ratio of 1:2 means one attack of the top layer played against two attacks of the bottom layer. Each layer uses an A major scale, moves in similar motion, begins with a sixth, and is in a 1:2 ratio.

Fig. 3.30. Counterpoint Diary Example 1

Example 2 uses the counterpoint characteristics of example 1, but the bottom layer is changed to a chromatic line. It also uses an open-A-string pedal.

Fig. 3.31. Counterpoint Diary Example 2

Example 3 takes example 2 and makes it into a single-note melody. Since the line is inspired by counterpoint, it is a good example of a compound line (see chapter 3).

Fig. 3.32. Counterpoint Diary Example 3

In example 4, the top layer uses diatonic sixths against a single-note line on the bottom, moving in contrary motion.

Fig. 3.33. Counterpoint Diary Example 4

Example 5 features repeating C to F triads moving over a descending line in C Mixolydian. It's fun separating chord symbols like this, to create interesting progressions.

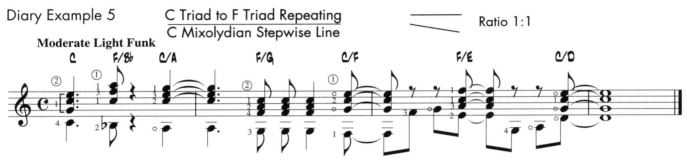

Fig. 3.34. Counterpoint Diary Example 5

Finally, in example 6, I use the triads from a standard tune, and place them against a descending chromatic line. There are other possibilities. Which chromatic line works? That's up to you.

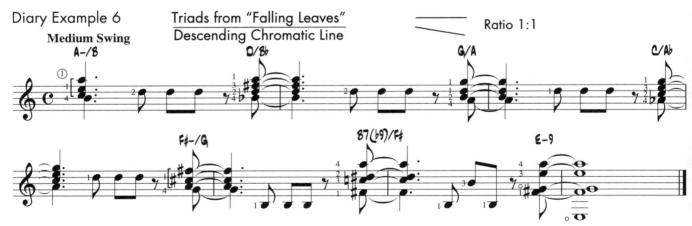

Fig. 3.35. Counterpoint Diary Example 6

The possibilities are limitless. Your diary will be a resource for your creative work as an improviser and composer. With a little work, you will find some interesting sounds. Start simple. I hope your diary grows fat with ideas.

Next are some counterpoint formulas for you to try. Sketch them in and play them. Let your imagination find other possibilities. Even try two keys at the same time. At first, it sounds crazy but you'll find some great ideas when you bring two simple ideas together.

So, here is your first sketch. You continue this one!

Your Diary Entry   G Major Scale Stepwise   unison   Ratio 1:1
                    G Major Scale Stepwise

Fig. 3.36. Your Diary Example 1

Try the same formula with a different ratio.

Your Diary Entry   G Major Scale Stepwise   unison   Ratio 1:2
                    G Major Scale Stepwise

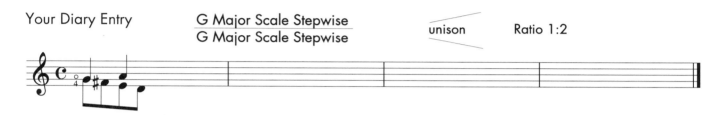

Fig. 3.37. Your Diary Example 2

If notes become too spread out for your taste or for your chops, continue the line in another octave. This, you may remember, is octave adjustment (see chapter 2). Notice here the B continues downward to an A, but now, it is an octave higher. Then, the E moves to D.

Fig. 3.38. Octave Adjustment

Regular diary entries will really expand on your observation abilities and get your compositional and improvisational imagination going. It's endless. And that's a good thing.

Again, this chapter is only the tip of many counterpoint possibilities. Counterpoint is always around. Not only in the dance of my pen with this paper, but also in *you* flipping through the pages of J.S. Bach's *Sonatas for Solo Violin* or Johann Fux's book mentioned earlier in this chapter. Or hearing counterpoint from Bill Evans, or John McLaughlin, or Andrés Segovia, or *YOU.*

You are a line of counterpoint when you perform with others. Apply all the techniques to yourself. Become cantus, become cambiata, contrary motion, tension, resolve, above, below, up, and down. The study of creative music is an endless joy. And that is another good thing!

Chapter 4   3-Note Chord Structures — The Palette Chart

"Three's company, four's a crowd"
—Naomi D. Anj

It was a hot day in July, 1995, and there it was: my first guitar, bought more than thirty years ago, staring at me. I hadn't seen it for about twenty-five years when I passed it to my nephew Doug, and while visiting his London flat, I became reacquainted with my first ax. It is a sunburst, acoustic, Harmony arch top, a $25 chunk of beauty! Playing it again brought back memories of the fun I had making new musical discoveries.

Over the years, I learned lots of chord forms and scales, and began soloing with licks gleaned from listening and transcriptions. I started to feel "in control." Then, with time, I noticed that the fun of discovery and surprise I felt with my first guitar was gone! I had learned lots of cool voicings, and 4- and 8-bar licks. But something was missing. I was so much "in control" that I was responding to chord symbols like one of Pavlov's salivating dogs. It was time to stir up my musical barrel of ideas.

I had many great musicians as teachers, and one common theme echoes from their teachings: simplicity. Less is more. So, I began to focus on simple, 3-note, melodic and harmonic structures. They are small enough to be flexible, yet large enough to have a distinctive character. Excitedly overwhelmed with possibilities, I developed what is now called the Palette Chart. It acts as a table of contents and a jumping-off point for 3-note explorations, and it is called the Palette Chart because it displays interesting harmonic and 3-note colors.

Why The Chart?

The Palette Chart was developed to organize 3-note harmonic and melodic structures, which are effective music building tools for the guitarist. Since many 3-note structures do not have clear chord symbol names, like their 4-, 5-, and 6-note chord colleagues, the chart is also a handy tool for naming them. Let's look at some of the benefits that these 3-note harmonic and melodic structures can give.

Some Benefits of 3-Note Structures

In chapter 2, the Palette Chart was introduced, and the power and flexibility of the 3-note melodic motif was explored. Now, let's see how 3-note chord structures can also add to our music resources. Using 3-note harmonic structures or chords adds nice contrast to the standard 4-, 5-, or 6-note harmonies. Because of their "lightness," they move more easily. Holding a 3-note structure frees fingers of the fingerboard hand, enabling more independent voice-motion possibilities. This added lightness also produces a transparency that enables the individual tone colors of each note to be heard more clearly.

Before moving into the details of the palette chart, here is the introduction to "Argentina," a composition in which I utilize 3-note structures. Listen how clearly the tone color of each note or voice comes through, and observe the flexible movement within the 3-note structures. Also notice how easy it is to play. An open A string is added for support.

Argentina (an excerpt)
A study in 3-note structures

Fig. 4.1. "Argentina" Intro

Check out how the Palette Chart works with this tune's 3-note chord structures.

The Palette Chart

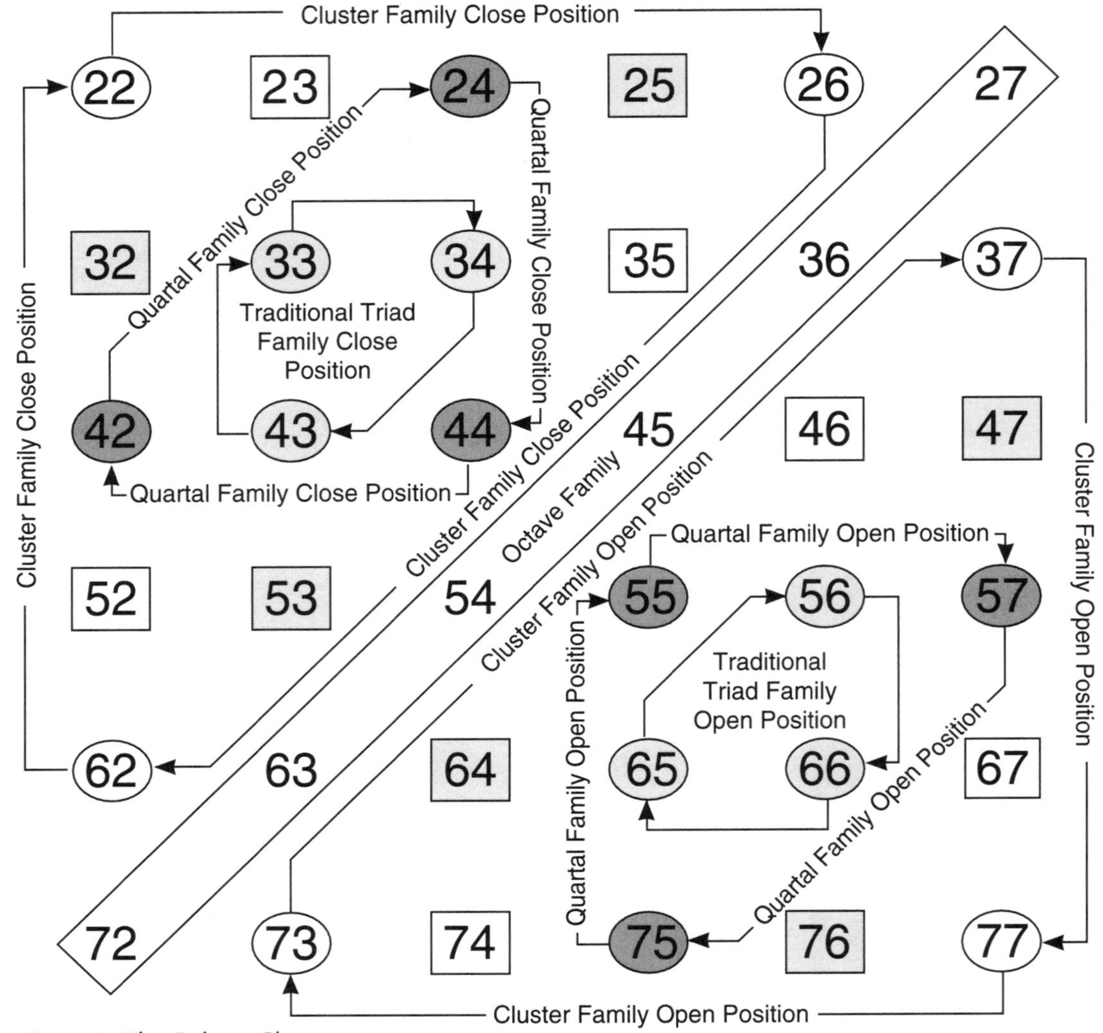

Fig. 4.2. The Palette Chart

Cluster Family seeds are in white ellipses.

Traditional Triad Family seeds are in light grey ellipses.

Quartal Family seeds are in dark grey ellipses.

Seventh Chords No Fifth Family seeds are in white boxes.

Seventh Chords No Third Family seeds are in grey boxes.

Octave Family seeds are in a diagonal box.

Looks Too Intellectual?

A question that often comes up when approaching fairly intellectual-looking topics like the Palette Chart is: What's with all those numbers?!

Just remember, many ideas or techniques that now feel pretty instinctive at one time probably seemed fairly intellectual—like all the chord forms you now know! And remember when you first looked at those little mysterious chord diagrams with the little dots? Or when your friend slowly talked you through that cool lick? It's up to you to chew on the intellectual stuff and get it to the point where it comes out instinctively. So here goes!

How The Palette Chart Works

The details of how the Palette Chart organizes 3-note melodic motifs were explained in chapter 2. Now, let's dive into the 3-note chord structures, which we can call "seeds," from now on. A 3-note seed (chord) consists of two intervals stacked together. The numbers in the chart represent these two "stacked" intervals. Take the 42 structure, as an example. It represents a seed consisting of a fourth with a second *stacked* on top of it. Remember, these intervals are diatonic (in the key) to the particular scale type one is building from.

Let's build some seeds using a C major scale for illustration. A 35 seed is built from the first note of the C major scale, C. The third (the 3 in 35) from C is created by stacking the note E, and the fifth (the 5 in 35) from E is produced by stacking the note B.

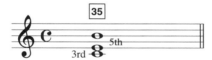

Fig. 4.3. A 35 Structure

Let's look at another seed from the Palette Chart: a 62 seed built on D, the second note of the C major scale. Create the sixth by stacking a B from the diatonic scale, and the second by stacking a C.

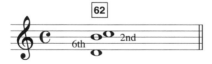

Fig. 4.4. A 62 Structure

Since we are working diatonically here, the quality of the seeds' intervals (perfect, minor, major, augmented, or diminished) depends on the scale degree and the scale type from which you are building. Here is a 44 seed, first stacked on a C major scale and then on a C harmonic minor scale.

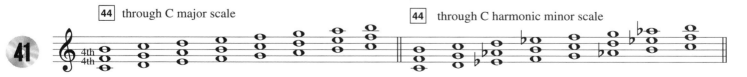

Fig. 4.5. Using 44 Seeds through C Major and C Harmonic Minor

The Interval Families of the Palette Chart

In the Palette Chart, each seed belongs to a particular interval family, such as the "Traditional Triads" family. They are connected to the rest of their family by shapes, colors, or arrows. Arrows indicate inversion directions.

The Traditional Triads family seeds are created by stacking thirds, producing the 33 seed, its inversions 34 and 43, and its open position forms 66, 65, and 56. (Inversions and open position are explained below.)

The Quartal family seeds are created by stacking diatonic fourths, producing the 44 seed, its inversions 42 and 24, and its open position forms 55, 57, and 75. The Cluster family seeds are stacked seconds, producing its 22 seed, its inversions 26 and 62, and open-position forms 77, 73, and 37.

Notice how the Cluster, Quartal, and Traditional Triad families are also connected by arrows, indicating the inversions, and then further labeled as being in open or close position. The other families are also connected visually by shape. The family Seventh Chords with No Fifth Degrees has white boxes around each seed. The family Seventh Chords with No Third Degree has gray boxes. The family connected within the long diagonal box is called the Octave family because there is an octave between the bottom and top notes of each of its seeds.

For further clarity and visual organization on the palette chart, color in each of the Traditional Triad family seeds with a light blue, the Quartal family yellow, the Cluster family light purple, and the Octave family a light green. Keep the Seventh Chords No Fifth and Seventh Chords No Third families as they are.

Again, a family consists of a seed and its inversions, in both close and open positions. Let's first look at how the families connect by inversion. Here is the Quartal Close family, illustrated in a C Dorian (B-flat major) scale. The family consists of the 44, 42, and 24 seeds. Inversions are created by restacking a seed's intervals, leapfrog-fashion, taking the seed's bottom note and bringing it up an octave, on top of the other two notes.

The Quartal Family Close-Position Inversions

Fig. 4.6. Quartals Close Inversions

Here is the Clusters Close family in all its inversions. Again, notice the leapfrogging of the bottom note to create the inversions. The 22 seed is a tough (if not impossible) finger-grabber without the occasional help of open strings. Its inversions, 26 and 62, are much easier to finger, and they retain the unique richness of the Cluster family.

The Cluster Family Close-Position Inversions

Fig. 4.7. Clusters Close Inversions

Close- and Open-Position Structures

The Palette Chart is divided in half diagonally by the Octave family. The close seed families are found in the upper-left triangle, and the open seed families are found in the lower-right triangle.

These terms *close* and *open* refer to how much room there is between the seeds' notes. In a close-position seed, the interval distance between the bottom and top notes is within an octave. Here are some close position seeds from the Palette Chart's upper-left triangle: a 24, a 23, and a 62 seed, in the key of E major. Notice the interval distance between the bottom and top notes is within an octave.

Some Close-Position Seeds

Fig. 4.8. A Variety of Close Seeds

To open up a close-position seed, bring the middle note up or down an octave, so that it is either above or below the seed's other two notes. In the next example, the seeds from the previous example change from a close position to an open position. Notice the middle note, moving above the seeds' other notes to "open" things up.

Close Position Moving to Open Position

The middle note of a close-position seed moves to an octave above to create an open-position seed. Open-position seeds span more than an octave between bottom and top notes.

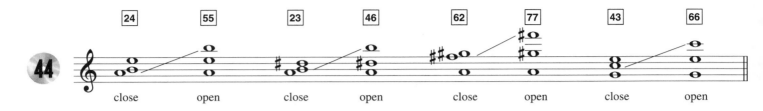

Fig. 4.9. A Variety of Close-to-Open Seeds

Spread Position

Moving a close-position seed's bottom voice down an octave produces a *spread position* seed.

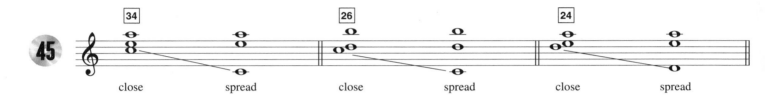

Fig. 4.10. A Variety of Close to Spread Seeds

Opening up the bottom of a seed, like this, is acoustically effective. Here is a simple passage that uses some spread seeds.

Fig. 4.11. Spread Seeds

Getting Started

The Palette Chart was introduced (chapter 2) as a directory for exploring 3-note melodic motifs. This is a good way to begin using it. Now, we'll begin our harmonic explorations. We'll start with the Traditional Triad family in close and open positions. Coloring them blue on the chart will make them easier to link, at a glance.

Traditional Triad Family

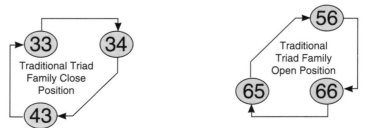

Fig. 4.12. Traditional Triads Family

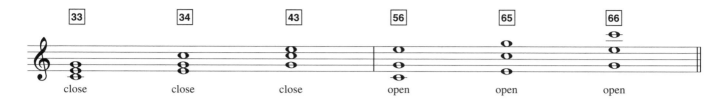

Fig. 4.13. Some Traditional Triads, Open and Close position, in C Major

Traditional Triads is a good family to begin with, since these structures state tonality (major or minor) clearly. Also, the other interval families' qualities are heard relative to this family. The lightness and flexibility of the 3-note harmonic structures are well illustrated with this family, as well.

These first studies will work with traditional harmonic chord progressions, but instead of interpreting the symbols as traditional chord forms, we will work with only the basic triads. Then, suspension notes moving into the triad notes from above and approach notes moving into the triad notes from below will be used to create a beautiful 3-part counterpoint.

In this first study, "Stella by Flashlight," each chord symbol's basic triad is written in a variety of open and close positions. (This will serve as a foundation for the upcoming suspension-approach study). The basic triads consist of the chord symbols' root, third, and fifth, or of the chord's third, fifth, and seventh degrees. The first bar uses a G minor triad, the basic triad built from the third, fifth, and seventh degree of the opening chord symbol, E–7(♭5).

Stella by Flashlight
Open and Close Position Traditional Triad Seeds
(Foundation for Suspension-Approach Study)

Fig. 4.14. Basic Triads, As Used in "Stella by Flashlight"

Now, let's take this "foundation" and put it into action. In the Suspension-Approach Study, an original note of the basic triad is approached, either from a step above (suspension) or from a step below (approach note). This creates a simple cadence, similar to the species two counterpoint studies in chapter three. For example, in bar 1, the top note of the first G minor triad is approached from a scale note above, and then the bottom note of the second G minor triad is approached from a scale note above. It continues with a series of approach notes from above and below any of the original triad's three notes.

For now, the rhythm is kept simple. Later, we will use some rhythmic variation and Double Combo Special to create more interest.

Compare the approach notes with the foundation study above (fig. 4.14).

Stella by Flashlight
Suspension-Approach Study

Fig. 4.15. Suspension-Approach
Study

Of course, the possibilities are vast. They will greatly add to your harmonic vocabulary, which is what this book is all about! How vast are the possibilities? Add them up; it's in the hundreds! Remember all the variables:

- You can use either of the chord symbol's basic triads.

- You can play this triad in either open or close position.

- You can choose any inversion you wish.

- You can approach any note of a triad from above or below!

The possibilities sure add up, and we're not even adding rhythmic or textural variety yet!

What I like most about this technique is that it makes me much less jealous of piano players. It has a "two-handed" sound, like a piano player playing a melody against a sustained chord.

It is also a nice accompaniment technique. To illustrate this, here is the first several bars of "Stella by Flashlight," with Double Combo Special (see chapter 3). As you may remember, in this technique, we use standard chord forms to support a new technique, such as this one, helping transition the new ideas into our playing.

Stella by Flashlight
Double Combo Special

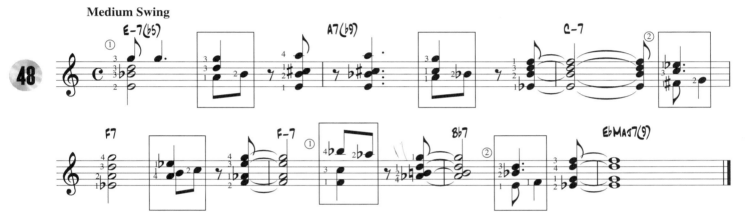

Fig. 4.16. "Stella By Flashlight" Double Combo Special. Boxes indicate suspension-approach technique.

Next are two choruses built on the jazz standard, "Giant Strides." The first chorus uses suspension-approach technique. The second chorus adds rhythmic variation, using the *same notes* as the first chorus. The rhythmic variations really enhance the feeling of three separate lines of counterpoint.

Giant Strides

Fig. 4.17a. "Giant Strides"
Chorus with Suspension-
Approach Study

Fig. 4.17b. "Giant Strides"
Chorus with Rhythmic Variations

Begin combining suspension-approach with rhythmic variation by sketching out examples, as I have done here. With time, it will be as accessible as any other technique you now have.

I began working with this technique because it introduces one of the guitar's really beautiful textures: polyphony (remember my birthday party back in chapter 2?). Once you begin working with polyphonic textures, it is hard to stop!

One Way To Learn All Those Darn Seeds!

Choose a seed, for example 44, and sketch out the seed on the fingerboard, as I have done on the Fingerboard Template (see figure 4.18). For starters, use a major scale (I use a C major scale in fig. 4.18). This template works as a visual guide to help you learn the shapes. Sketch the seed, going diatonically up the scale along the strings. Continue it on all possible sets of strings, as shown in fig. 4.18. In Foundations (chapter 6), there are blank fingerboard templates for you to copy and use to fill in the seeds you are studying. I made templates for all the seeds and they really help in my explorations.

Make your own templates for all the palette chart seeds from the blank template in Foundations (chapter 6).

44 on G, B, and High E Strings

◄— Pegboard

Frets: 1   2   3   4   5   6   7   8   9   10   11   12   13   14   15

44 on D, G, and B Strings

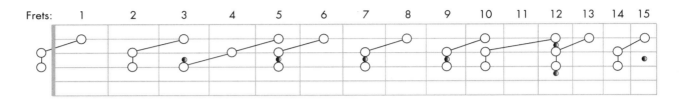

44 on A, D, and G Strings

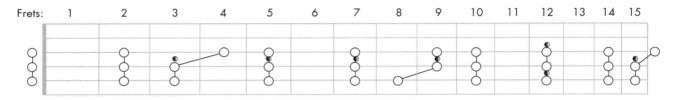

44 on Low E, A, and D Strings

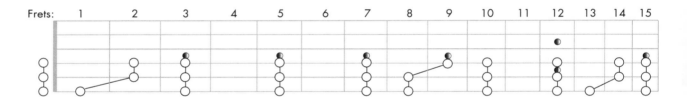

Fig. 4.18. Templates for 44 Seeds

Thickened Melody and Pandiatonicism

Some of the Palette Chart families can be described using common chord symbols—Traditional Triads, Seventh Chords No Fifth, and so on. Other families do not have such common symbols, such as Clusters.

Though they may not fit the standard chord notation, they complement traditional chords very well, and are nice colors to use in composition and improvisation. But when can they be used in relation to a chord symbol?

First, don't think of the seed families only as chords. Think of them as interval colors that can be used to "thicken" a single-note line or melody. Use seeds as you would use notes from a scale to build a single-note line. As with notes from a scale, the notes in the seed should all respect the chord symbol. Are the seed's notes basic chord tones? Non-chord notes? Is one a strong tension note relative to the chord symbol?

Pandiatonicism means that all (pan) notes in the key (diatonic) are considered equal, and do not follow the traditional harmonic "hierarchy." In the classical world, the invention of this concept has been a powerful one. Basically, it means to consider the entire chord scale as possible material for comprovisation.

This more "linear" attitude opens up a lot of rhythmic and contrapuntal possibilities. Here are two examples.

The first uses a 44 seed from the Quartal family, through an A Dorian scale (G major notes). The chords are used to "thicken" the single-note line, adding color and textural interest. The single-note line also uses Quartal family motifs of 44 (bar 1) and 24 (bar 5).

The second example uses the Cluster family seed 26 as transition between the more standard chord forms. They are a nice color here.

Two Thickened Melody and Pandiatonicism Examples
A Quartal Family Study

Example 1

Liten Vals
A Cluster Family Study

Fig. 4.19. Two Examples
of Thickening and
Pandiatonicism

The Quartal Family

Through the music of Palestrina, Claude Debussy, McCoy Tyner, and countless others, quartal harmony (chords stacked in fourths) has become quite a familiar sound. In the Palette Chart, the Quartal family is represented by the 44, 24, and 42 close-position seeds and the 55, 57, and 75 open-position seeds. Earlier, you may have colored the members of this family yellow.

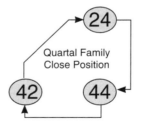

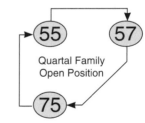

Fig. 4.20. Quartal Family

The Quartal Family Notated in F Dorian
First in Close Position, Then in Open Position

Fig. 4.21. Quartals Notated

Compare the sound of the Quartal family to the sound of the Traditional Triad family. With quartals, the presence of major or minor tonality is less clear.

A traditional triad seed with its third degree suspended (or lowered) produces a quartal seed. Since the quartal structure is less tonally implicit, it can be more efficient, in certain situations. Debussy and his Impressionistic buddies were essentially looking for harmonic devices that were less traditionally motivated. Pandiatonicism and quartal harmony became popular new sounds. In the jazz world, the same harmonic revolution occurred, as is evident in Gil Evans and John Coltrane's modal explorations, and McCoy Tyner's support to John Coltrane's solos.

For our own Quartal family explorations, let's start with a simple modal melody, and use the Quartal family in some thickened melody variations. Here are some possibilities.

First the melody.

The Simple D Dorian Melody

Fig. 4.22. Modal Melody

Diatonic Thickening

Now, thicken the melody using a 44 seed (all notes in D Dorian).

Here is the simple melody thickened with 44 seeds.

Fig. 4.23. Modal Melody 44 Seed

Exchange of Inversions

Next, alternate between two inversions of the close-position quartal seeds, 24 and 44. Observe how the voice motion under the melody becomes more interesting here than with using only one seed (as in example 4.23).

Here is an exchange between the 24 and 44 seeds.

Fig. 4.24. Exchange of Inversions

Parallel Thickening

Here is a variation using the 44 seed. Now, instead of moving diatonically under the melody, the 44 will move *parallel*. The intervals of the 44 seed remain *exactly* the same or equidistant—a perfect fourth and a perfect fourth, from structure to structure.

This introduces some non-diatonic notes (notice the F-sharp in the third structure), which is part of the charm of parallel motion.

Here is a use of parallel motion under the melody, all perfect fourths.

Fig. 4.25. Parallel Thickening

Double Parallel Thickening

In *double parallel thickening*, we alternate between two seeds, keeping each of them *parallel to themselves.* Here is an exchange between a 24 (major second and perfect fourth) seed and a 44 (augmented fourth and perfect fourth) seed. Again, notice the non-diatonic notes.

Here is double parallel motion under the melody.

Fig. 4.26. Double Parallel

The parallel and double parallel techniques are pretty powerful, and they can be just the right ideas to heat up a modal situation where the tonality is static (not moving).

Remember, these are just some possibilities. Find more and send me some!

Here is an example using the Quartal family along with standard chord forms. This is primarily diatonic thickening here, with an occasional chromatic approach (bars 12 and 14).

57

Just Fiends
Double Combo Special with Quartal Seeds

Fig. 4.27. Quartal Study

This next example is a chorus using quartal seeds, only without standard chord forms. Without the standard chord forms, the tonalities are more subtle, which is part of the quartal family's personality. This technique is more difficult since it is easy to lose the intention of the original progression.

Another Sunny Tune
A Study with Quartals Only

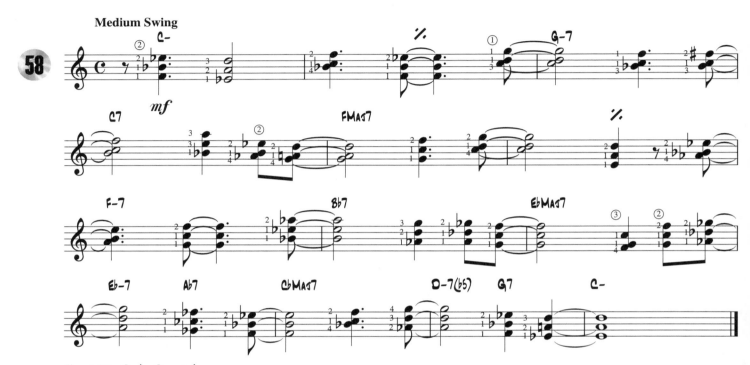

Fig. 4.28. Only Quartals

The Open-Position Quartals

The Open-Position Quartal seeds have the power interval, the fifth. They can be used effectively either gently or in power mode. This short example was conceived as being fairly gentle. I added open E and A strings as pedals, creating depth under the Open-Position Quartal seeds.

An Open-Position Quartal-Seed Study

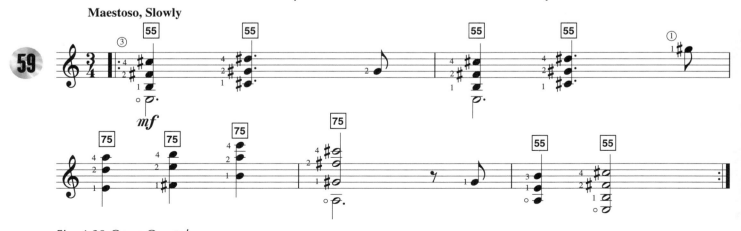

Fig. 4.29 Open Quartals

Again, the possibilities are too extensive to cover here. These are just some seeds to inspire you. It's up to you to do the watering!

Say, why not try a suspension-approach study with Quartals, as we did with Traditional Triads? Try it on your own!

Another Way to Learn Those Darn Seeds!

Go to Ears 3 in Foundations (chapter 6) for a cool study to help in familiarizing yourself with the seeds and really get them into your belly. Oh, and there is a scratch and sniff there, too, to check out!

The Cluster Family

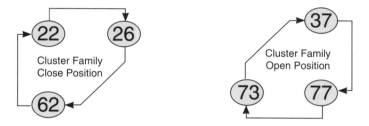

Fig. 4.30. The Cluster Family Notated

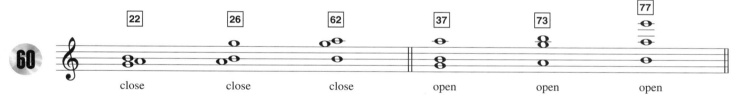

Fig. 4.31. Clusters Notated

Clusters, as in grapes (color this family light purple on the palette chart), refers to the closeness of the notes in this family's seeds, since they are built using seconds (see the first seed in Figure 4.31). Playing this 22 seed on the guitar without using open strings is very difficult or impossible, but its inversions (26 and 62) and open forms (77, 73, and 37) are much easier. The Cluster family works nicely alongside standard forms, as seen in Liten Vals, earlier in this chapter. The Cluster seeds are also a nice contrast to the other seeds.

Use the templates to help you learn to play the Cluster family, or any family, as you did earlier with the quartals. Here is a 26-Cluster seed template to help you begin studying the Cluster family.

26 Template
26 on G, B, and High E Strings

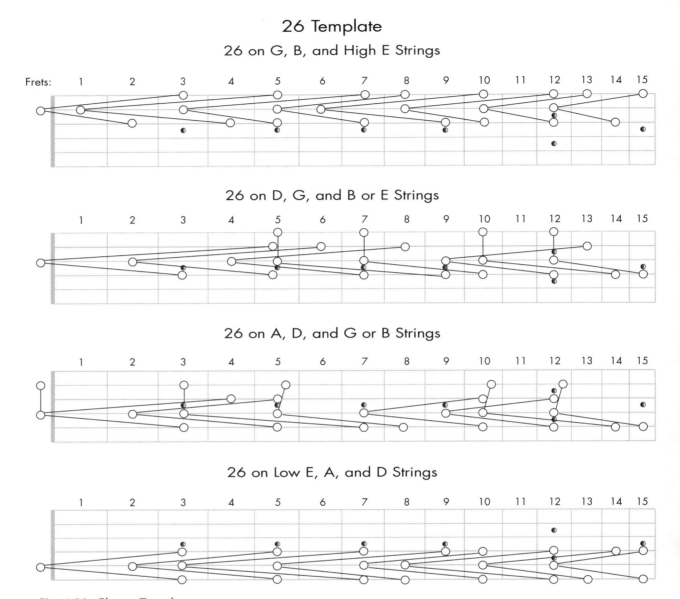

26 on D, G, and B or E Strings

26 on A, D, and G or B Strings

26 on Low E, A, and D Strings

Fig. 4.32. Cluster Template

Clusters from Sustained Scales

For our first Cluster family study, let's kill two birds with one stone. We'll find some Cluster sounds and work on our octave-adjustment chops (skills) at the same time.

Each Cluster seed is simply three notes connected by seconds. Of course, the inversions and open-position seeds spread these notes out a bit, but the same notes are always at play. So, for the first Cluster study, let's use a simple scale, moving in seconds.

If you went to a piano, held down the sustain pedal, and played the first three notes of a C major scale, you'd create a Cluster sound. Let's try that on the guitar. Of course, we have no sustain pedal, so we will just hold down our fingers, allowing the three notes to ring together. For this example, we'll need an open E string for the E.

Let Ring

Fig. 4.33. Sustaining C, D, and E

If we tried this with the first three notes of a C minor scale—C, D, and E-flat— we'd be in trouble, unless we put the E-flat in another octave. That is what this really cool study is all about.

Let Ring

Fig. 4.34. Sustaining C, D, and E-Flat

Play the C major scale, and with the help of octave adjustment, have every three notes of the scale sustain, creating a 3-note-Cluster seed. Here is an example of a C major scale using this technique. Again, sustain each 3-note group, and notice that each group consists of three consecutive scale notes.

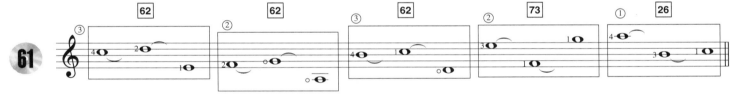

Fig. 4.35. Sustained Scales Study

This really works for learning Cluster family seed shapes. It can also yield some very pretty comprovisational ideas.

Clusters from Chord Symbols

As you can hear, the Cluster family has a distinctive sound-color personality. The Cluster family can capture a clear major or minor tonality, since an interval of a third (or its inversion, the sixth) is always present.

Here is another technique to help you find some Cluster sounds and some Cluster-like sounds (there is only one second in these seeds). It will help you capture a chord symbol's progression or cadence objective.

Below is a simple progression of two chords, E7 to A–7, with their related scales (chord scales) below them. The filled-in notes in each scale will not be used in the Cluster-chord study because they are strong non-chord tones, which would destroy the chords' motion or function. Some folks call them "avoid notes," which is misleading because in certain musical situations, they would sound great. But in the general chord-progression world, they are "no-no" notes.

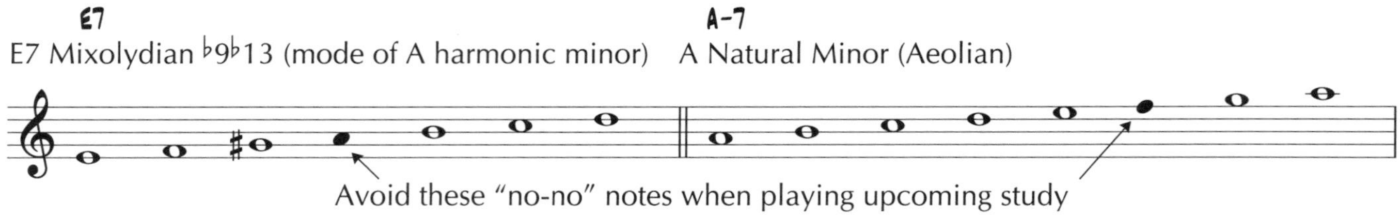

E7
E7 Mixolydian ♭9♭13 (mode of A harmonic minor)   **A–7**
A Natural Minor (Aeolian)

Avoid these "no-no" notes when playing upcoming study

Fig. 4.36. E7 to A–7

This simple technique will help you find lots of Cluster sounds relative to a chord symbol.

1. Sketch out the symbol's scale, as illustrated above.

2. Grab any two neighboring notes (except the "no-no" note) from the chord scale. For the E7 chord above, I chose the E and the F from the scale.

Two notes chosen from scale of chord symbol

E7
E7 Mixolydian ♭9♭13 (mode of A harmonic minor)

Fig. 4.37. E and F

3. If the third degree of the chord symbol is not in the two notes chosen, then add it to complete the cluster.

Third degree of chord symbol added

E7
E7 Mixolydian ♭9♭13 (mode of A harmonic minor)

Fig. 4.38. E, F, and G-Sharp

4. If the third degree is present, as with these two notes from the A minor scale, add the root as the third note. If the chord symbol is a dominant-7 chord, you could add the flat 7, as another option.

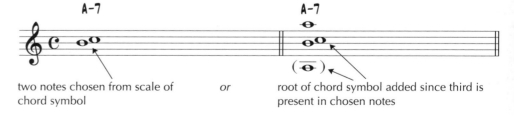

two notes chosen from scale of   *or*   root of chord symbol added since third is
chord symbol   present in chosen notes

Fig. 4.39. B and C and B, C, and A

Again, this is only a jumping-off point. Not all of the structures you find are guaranteed to please, just as with anything in music!

Here are a couple of examples with clusters derived from chord symbols. The first is basically a "rhythm changes" progression. The clusters produce a pretty clear harmonic direction in this example, thanks to the presence of the third degrees in the cluster seeds. The thirds are darkened, for illustration purposes.

Cluster Study with Rhythm Changes
Darkened notes indicate third degrees.

Fig. 4.40. "Rhythm Changes" Clusters

Here is another example. The third is used less here, which creates a more subtle quality of motion.

Cluster Study in C

Fig. 4.41. Progression in C Major. Less use of thirds here produces a more subtle tonal effect. Thirds are darkened for illustration.

The Other Palette Chart Families

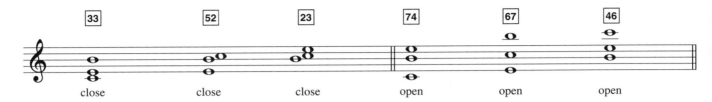

Fig. 4.42. Seventh Chords No
Fifths. Notated in close position,
then in open position, in C major.

Harmonizing Bass Lines

The Seventh Chords No Fifth (degree) family has clear tonal sound. They are lighter weight than the standard chord forms, making them flexible elements of an accompaniment. One essential technique these seeds are great for is walking bass lines with chords—essentially "thickening" *above* the bass melody or line. The 35 and 74 seeds are most used in this technique, as are the traditional triads in open position (65, 66, and 56).

Let's thicken up a simple bass line on a G7 chord. Let's say it is the first bar of a 12-bar blues in G.

A Simple Bass Melody for G7

Fig. 4.43. Bass Line Only

This line is a good one to start with because it has *all* the possible note relationships against a chord symbol: basic chord tones and passing tones (diatonic and chromatic). The first and last quarter notes are basic chord tones of the G7 chord—the root G and the third degree B. The quarter note A on beat 2 is a diatonic passing tone, and the A-sharp on beat 3 is a chromatic passing tone. Any note of a bass line you are harmonizing will come under one of these categories.

Let's thicken up the bass line with some Seventh Chord No Fifth seeds and Open-Traditional-Triad seeds. We'll refer to this example as The Lick.

The Lick

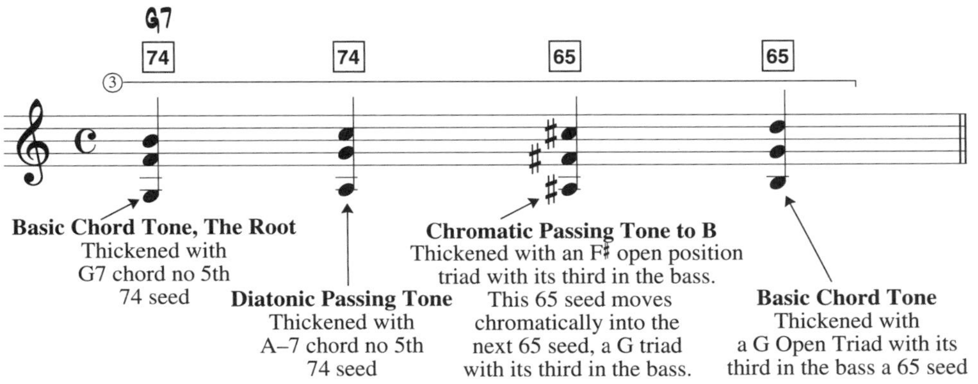

Fig. 4.44. The Lick

Now that "The Lick" is ready to go, let's look at the next bar of the G blues, with the C7 chord. For now, let's use "The Lick" again, but starting on C7. Bring "The Lick" up to the eighth fret to play it. Or else, you could play it with the bottom voice on the A string; this will give you another spot to play "The Lick," which may give you more efficiency of motion.

The Lick on the A string

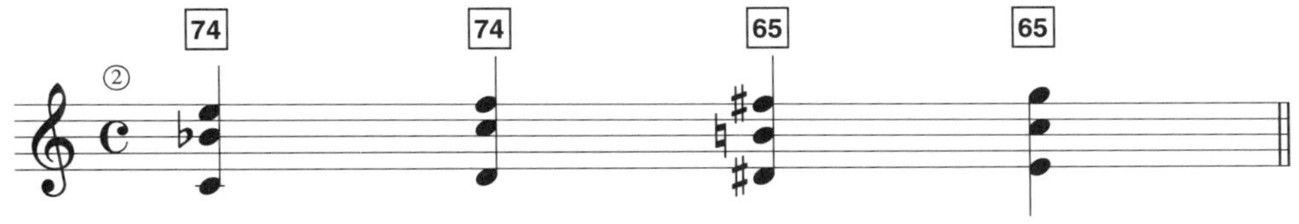

Fig. 4.45. The Lick on A string

Continue "The Lick" through the rest of the G7 blues form, building your fingerboard hand's confidence. You can also use "The Lick" for major 7 chords; just change the seventh in the first structure to a major seventh instead of a flat seventh!

Before we explore harmonizing other types of bass lines, let's work on our strumming hand. Some folks would play these harmonized ideas with only their fingers, others would use only their pick, and others would use both pick and fingers. I suggest getting used to all these possibilities. Each of these has their own unique sound personalities.

Here are some finger studies for the strumming hand. First, we use our good old friend, "The Lick," playing the seeds' bass notes (bottom notes) and chord notes (top two notes) rhythmically together. Then, play the "bass note" first, followed by the chords. Then, the chords first, followed by the bass note. Then mix up these techniques. It will help to give more independence of sound between the bass and the chord. Again, play through this study with pick and fingers, then play it with only pick, and then with only fingers.

Some Strumming-Hand Variations with "The Lick"

Fig. 4.46. Right-Hand Variations

Now that "The Lick" is driving us mad, let's harmonize some other bass lines.

Remember that each bass note will either be a basic chord tone, a diatonic passing tone, or a chromatic passing tone.

As you may have noticed, each bass note thus far has been harmonized. This was done so that you have the option of putting a harmony to any bass note you wish. Harmonizing every bass note is not always the best musical decision, so the following example will try to be a bit more "musical," and use unharmonized bass notes here and there.

In the harmonized bass lines below, the diatonic and chromatic passing tones are labeled in parentheses. Remember, each bass note is harmonized as a basic chord tone, a diatonic passing tone, or a chromatic passing tone. Be sure to listen to bass players for great walking bass melodies to harmonize.

Some More Harmonized Bass Line Possibilities

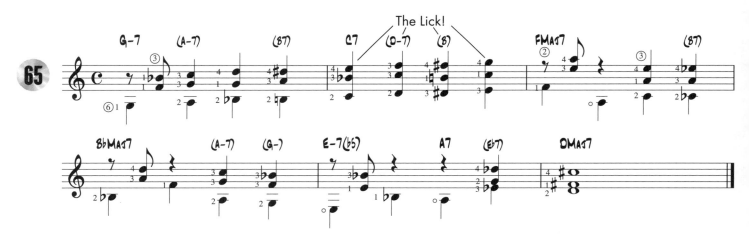

Fig. 4.47. More Bass Line Possibilities

The Octave Family

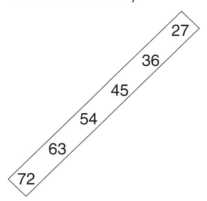

Fig. 4.48. Octave Family

The Octave Family Notated

Fig. 4.49. Octave Family Notated

The Octave family's 3-note seeds are really only two different notes, the third note being an octave doubling of the seed's bottom note. These seeds are an octave "in height," or in the distance between their bottom and top notes. Color this family a light green on the Palette Chart.

These are effective melody thickeners, as you can hear in the talents of George Benson. Here is another section of "Argentina," the piece that opened this chapter. The 63 seed is used throughout.

"Argentina" Excerpt
Using Octave Family 63 Seeds

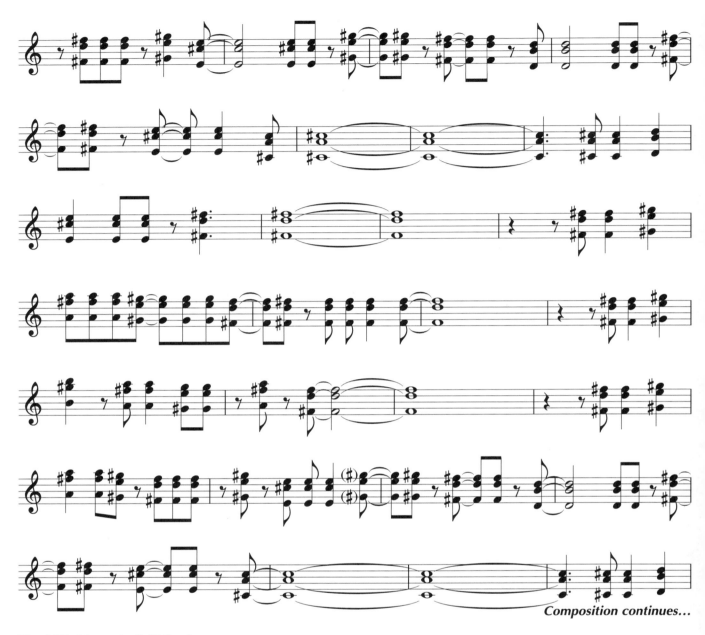

Composition continues...

Fig. 4.50. "Argentina" 63 Section

I hope this chapter has inspired you to pursue the land of 3-note chord structures more fully. It introduces some of the possibilities of the Palette Chart. I really have to stop now, because if I continued with more palette chart ideas like the Magic Hybrid Chart and the Super Duper Double Whammy Chromium Platinum Chart, they would be too mind-boggling. I'll have to put them in my next book.

You might ask, why is there no chapter in this book about standard 4-, 5-, and 6-note chord forms, including hybrid chords and upper-structure triads? Two reasons. First, there are skillions of books, chord dictionaries, and theory books already written on these topics. And second, I have too many ideas concerning standard chord forms, especially about ways to breathe new life into those suckers. So, those ideas will have to wait for yet another book, with the help of God.

Chapter 5   Form

"Form is the balance

between tension and

relaxation."

—Ernst Toch

I would like to give credit to another of my greatest teachers—actually, a performance group that I have been a part of for a while called the Creative Workshop. You already met them in chapter 1, with their rendition of *The Coronation*. The Creative Workshop is a performance workshop at the Berklee College of Music in Boston. Part of the Workshop's basic philosophy is compositional self-sufficiency; all pieces we perform are composed by workshop members. Inspiration for our compositions comes from many sources, including stories, poetry, and paintings. We also explore music philosophies, such as Arnold Schoenberg's tone rows and John Cage's aleatoric concepts, as well as traditional forms, such as the 12-bar blues. For notation, we may use traditional notation, graphics, text, or even objects, such as a flower or a dancer. Once, we had a goldfish as "conductor" for a piece, but the fish died just before the concert. I'm serious! A documentation of the Workshop's works and ideas, over its ten-years' existence, would make a compelling volume.

The most important lesson I have learned from the Workshop is that potential forms for our music are all around us. This chapter began with the quote from Ernst Toch. Of all the definitions of form that I have seen, Toch's seems the most alive and breathing. In the Workshop, I have found that the most successful compositions and improvisations are those built upon forms that breathe. For example, the language forms, such as poetry, haiku, and stories, are forms alive with the cadences (movement from tension to relaxation) inherent in their phrases and sentences. Their underall and overall forms exhibit a growth towards climax and release.

Form and cadence have already been discussed throughout this book, from the powerful sound dimensions, to the concepts of motif and "rebound effect" in single and compound lines, to counterpoint. Also, the phrase "repetition, contrast, and return" has been illustrated throughout. These elements are all part of *overall* form. They are the *underall* forms that reflect inner cadences. When put into play, working together, they produce the final composition.

This chapter will discuss and illustrate some user-friendly form ideas that can inspire your improvisation or your compositions. We don't always need to consciously think of a particular form before beginning an improvisation or composition. The art of "stream of consciousness"—just letting stuff instinctively happen—can be the most efficient way to go. And let's face it, that's where all creative musics began, before folks began defining things—pure inspiration, the best source. But there are times when our inspirations can use a jumpstart—a spark or catalyst (again, what this book is all about) to get things going. That goes for overall form as well.

When our instincts are working well, we naturally include repetition, contrast, and return, the basic elements found in many forms, such as basic song form (or ternary form AABA), and even sonata form. I don't have to list here the number of compositions that have been built from song form alone. The following piece was composed in a stream-of-consciousness mode (pure-instinct mode). After completing it, I realized that it was essentially in a basic song form, but with a twist. This piece is called "Rosie," and was composed in dedication to my mom. Let's give a listen to it first, and then we'll look at a brief analysis. I made this piece short and sweet, since Rosie was too.

Rosie
For My Mother

Jon Damian

Fig. 5.1. "Rosie"

Let's look at the overall form from the inside out, from the view of the underall forms (motifs, phrases etc.). The opening bars begin with a simple motif, beginning on the note E. It is a simple line, with a chromatic line rising as counterpoint, and some pedals of A and D for support.

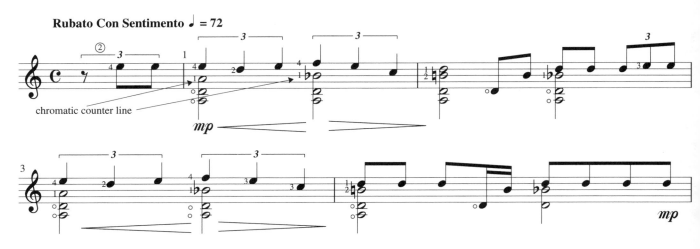

Fig. 5.2. "Rosie" Bars 1 to 4

This motif repeats in bar 5, starting with a D-natural (down a whole step) with some new chromatic counterpoint in bars 5 to 8. We'll call bars 1 to 8 the first "musical sentence" (since it comes to a rest or a "period"), or the *A section* of the form. In bar 9, the motif begins again, from the note F, but with the same counterpoint used in the opening. The repetition of the counterpoint and the new starting note, F, creates momentum.

Fig. 5.3. "Rosie" Bars 9 to 12

This phrase continues to bar 16 and cadences. Since this phrase is similar enough to the first section but not exactly, let's call this section *A¹* (*A section, variation 1*). At bar 17, the motif is played again, a bit faster, now starting on a B-flat, building more momentum with the register change. This phrase cadences at bar 31. Again, because of its similarity, let's call this section *A²* (*A section variation 2*). The next section moves higher still, starts on a C in A-flat major, and uses a contrasting motif. Since my Momma Rose was a beautiful Italiana lady, I used the quodlibet technique (see chapter 2) here, borrowing the first six notes of that old Italian favorite, "Arrividerci Roma." This phrase is called section *B* since it contrasts with the A sections. Bar 39 returns to the opening motif, but now in the middle voice, down an octave. It begins the descent towards the ending section, the coda (at bar 54), which consists of simple chords. This last section can be called *A³* (*A section, variation 3*). So, the overall form is this:

$$A \quad A^1 \quad A^2 \quad B \quad A^3$$

It is like a basic AABA form, but with a bit of a stutter on those A sections.

Working from Standard Progression Forms

This next form technique builds ideas using a set harmonic formula or *progression*. In previous chapters, standard harmonic progressions have been used to illustrate particular techniques. Now, the techniques will be combined—motifs through single note lines, counterpoint ideas, canons, 3-note structures—a free variety of textures from which to build and compose.

Here are some ideas using the harmonic progression from the A section of "Falling Leaves" as a basic cadential form. A combination of techniques are illustrated. Besides tapping the progression's overall cadential formula, the techniques used, such as 2-part counterpoint and suspension-approaches, produce strong underall form because of their inherent cadences. (See previous chapters for details concerning any of these techniques.)

Here is the first section of "Falling Leaves," followed by a reiteration (a repetition) spiced up with rhythmic variation and some added notes for linear motion. Observe the simple canon in bars 3 and 4. When using this technique as compositional form, the chord symbols should be an underlying cadential guide and are not meant to be played with this written material. The piece is intended for solo guitar.

Falling Leaves
With a Combination of Techniques

Fig. 5.4. Falling Leaves

Next is a developmental technique in which ideas are *inverted* (turned upside down). Listen to the upside-down variation of "Falling Leaves." The top lines essentially move to become the bottom lines and the bottom lines become the top. This technique can produce really nice ideas, and you may like them better than the original. This technique is a good example of utilizing existing materials in development. Again, the chord symbols are guides, not intended to be played.

Falling Leaves Inverted

Fig. 5.5. "Falling Leaves" Inverted

Often, folks think that composition and/or improvisation is like a waterfall of new ideas cascading towards the listener. Actually, the great composers and improvisers, from Duke Ellington to Ernst Toch (who the hell is he?) to Ornette Coleman, are ingenious recyclers of musical materials. This can be a very efficient and effective way to go.

Let's try some *Fireworks!* as our developmental technique in this next example. As you remember from chapter 1, *Fireworks!* is a technique in which elements of an idea are removed to create a new variation. We could use this technique to produce a nice introduction to precede the previous "Falling Leaves" variations, and also an ending. I often suggest to my students that they "work backwards" when building their compositions. This does make sense; how can you compose something that supposedly goes somewhere if you don't already know where it's going? Maybe that's how mystery writers do it?

Here is "Falling Leaves" put through some serious *Fireworks!* The original notes on beat 2 (bars 1 to 3) were removed.

I also squeezed in another technique called *retrograde*—literally, turning an idea backwards! Bars 8 to 12 are the notes of bars 1 to 7 backwards. Rhythms were changed a bit to protect the innocent.

Fig. 5.6. "Falling Leaves" with
Fireworks! and Retrograde

This final variation is simply a monophonic interpretation of "Falling
Leaves." Again, originally working with 2-part counterpoint ideas and
suspension-approaches, the variation is evident in the compound line
produced here.

Fig. 5.7. "Falling Leaves"
Monophonic

The variations illustrated above are not only examples for thematic development, but are also components of a form called *cyclique*—a form built
entirely upon statement of a theme at the beginning, followed by variations, such as upside-down and retrograde. So we're legit!

It is fun to work with the standard harmonic progression as a basic form,
and it is okay—even desirable—if your final solo piece eventually doesn't
capture the harmonic intent of the original progression. In fact, in official
"form jargon," the *variation* is a form in which the original theme becomes
unrecognizable! So, the original progression is only a spark for your work.
Of course, if you are using these techniques to create an accompaniment, a
clear reflection of the progression's harmonic intent is important.

Pure Shape Forms

In general music language, the word cadence is generally thought of in harmonic progression terms, like II-V-I. Let's take a common progression and use it to inspire non-harmonic cadential ideas. We'll use a II-V-I progression for the first harmonic idea. A simple analysis would be.

SD   D   T

II   V   I

T refers to *tonic* or "restful sound," D means *dominant* or "really unrestful sound," and SD refers to *subdominant* or "a sound somewhere between T and D."

So, the II-V-I starts simmering with the II chord, moves to a real sizzle with the V chord, than poops out, coming to a rest with the I chord. If I sketched this cadential activity graphically, it might look like this. (I used that scratchboard technique discussed in chapter 1 here, and with Blueshape coming up, it was fun to do.)

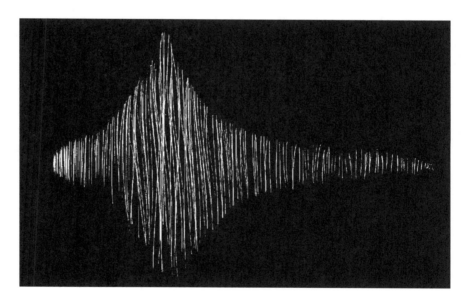

Fig. 5.8. II-V-I Scratchboard

With the II-V-I progression represented in purely graphical terms, its shape can be used easily to inspire cadences that are not of harmonic origin, such as rhythm, dynamics, and so on. So, look at the shape, left to right, and imagine some sounds that would move in this cadence.

How about these...

The II-V-Is of life!

A Sentence:

II   V   I

The girl swam to the dock.

A Sneeze:

ₐₐₐₐhhhhh**CH**Ooooooₒₒₒₒ.......

Or a really nice stretch or yawn in the

ₘₒᵣₙingah**h**hhhhₕₕₕₕₕ.......

Or a toilet flushing (sorry to be gross)

ₖₐₗU**NKAS**PLA**S**Hₕₕₕₕₕ.......

I am sure that you can think of lots more.

Now, look at the graphic image, or simply imagine it, and play a simple improv that moves with the intensities of the shape. DON'T LITERALLY PLAY A II-V-I. *THAT'S NOT THE POINT HERE!* Use dynamics, cadence, or rhythmic intensities, or articulation intensities, or interval intensities, or combinations of the above. Let the shape last for a few seconds. Try a minute-long improv based on the shape!

Blueshape

Next, we will utilize a tried and true form—the basic three-chord 12-bar blues—to inspire some improvisation and composition resources. The cadential rhythm of this progression is really beautiful, as you will see when we create the blueshape. First, let's analyze the 12-bar form, as we did with the II-V-I shape. Below, see the sketch of the blues progression with a graphic image, like we did with the II-V-I progression.

$\frac{4}{4}$ ‖: | T E7 | SD A7 | | T E7 | ⁄. | SD A7 | ⁄. | T E7 | ⁄. | D B7 | SD A7 | T E7 | D B7 | :‖ *next chorus continues...*

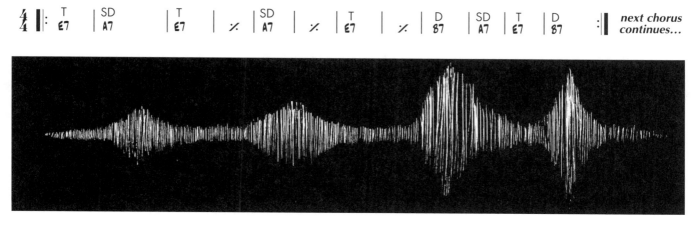

Fig. 5.9. Blueshape Scratchboard

Now that the blues progression is this funny-looking seismographic/EKG-looking shape, we can interpret it any way we want and tap its cadential magic.

Move your finger slowly along the blueshape image, from left to right. As you do imagine a solo dancer, on stage, moving to the changing intensities of the image. Okay? Let's go! Don't be shy, try it, you'll like it!

Next, move your finger along the shape, but imagine a full orchestra playing an imaginary composition that moves with the shape. Go through it as many times as you like. Move along the shape imagining a rocky seacoast, the rhythm and intensity of the waves moving to the shape. Can you feel the image's beautiful cadential rhythm, and the balance and symmetry between its points of rest and non-rest?

Stand up (I like doing this with the Creative Workshop), and do a pseudo-Tai-Chi series of moves following the intensities of the graphic image.

Then, as we did with the II-V-I shape, play an improv that moves with the blueshape and *NOT* a blues! Again, move any way you wish. Just begin, and move your idea through the series of intensities that the shape suggests.

> **Imagine yourself to be a flamenco guitarist playing a big old E major chord. Move your strumming hand rhythmically to the intensities of the blueshape.**

What I like most about this approach is that it gives an actual breathing-in-and-out form as a guide, instead of a lifeless series of letters to follow. As before, let the blueshape last as long or as short as you wish. Try delivering a joke or making a political speech that moves in its intensities.

The blues form is timeless. One important reason for its power is the cadential rhythm that we feel when we work with the blueshape.

One small point. This might sound too mathematical, but look at the length of the blueshape, from left to right, and find its climax point (where the shape really goes wild at the V chord). This climax point falls right on something called the *golden mean* or *golden section*—an asymmetrical balance point and natural ratio, found in the natural world and in the arts.

This point, approximately the two-thirds point in the life of a composition or improvisation, is considered a "balanced" point to have a high point or climax. You can more fully explore this phenomenon of form in a really cool book, *The Power Of Limits: Proportional Harmonies in Nature, Art and Architecture,* by Gyorgy Doczi (Shambhala Press).

Good luck with blueshape. Try shaping an entire solo or composition with this technique. It's just one of many possibilities.

Rows

In chapter 4, we discussed *pandiatonicism*, the technique in which all the diatonic notes of a scale are considered equal. The composer Arnold Schoenberg adapted this concept into something similar; he made all the notes of the chromatic scale equal by organizing them into *tone rows*. A *row* is a progression of events, like a chord progression, or in the case of Schoenberg's tone rows, a series of note events. Schoenberg originally introduced the tone row early in the twentieth century to act as essential underlying form for atonal composition. *Atonal* means that there is no tonality or key center. The tone row consists of a series of twelve different pitches, using the entire chromatic scale with no note repetitions. The composer would use this series or row to build a composition, maintaining the specific order of the tone row in its original form, as well as variations of the form such as *retrograde* (backwards) and *inversion* (upside down), or both (backwards and upside down). Here is Schoenberg's original row and its variations used in his *Suite for Piano, Opus 25.*

Fig. 5.10. Original tone row and variations from Arnold Schoenberg's Suite for Piano, Op. 25

For further studies in twelve-tone technique, refer to a cool book, *Composition Using All Twelve Tones,* by Josef Rufer, a student of Schoenberg.

Since *The Guitarist's Guide to Composing and Improvising* is designed for the guitarist as improviser as well as composer, I would like to introduce a new row technique. It was developed to be more accessible for the improviser than twelve-tone row concept. It is also very nice for the composer, as well. I call these *Interval Rows*.

Interval Rows

Instead of twelve note events, as in Schoenberg tone rows, I prefer using only three events, and in the case of interval rows, these events are intervals, rather than notes. An interval row consists of three different intervals.

For variety and interest, in my interval rows, I prefer to choose an interval from each of the three interval groups: the *tertials* (thirds and sixths), the *quartals* (fourths and fifths), and the *secundals* (seconds and sevenths). This also assures both dissonant and consonant possibilities for cadences. Here is an interval row that meets these specs, so let's use it for some variations.

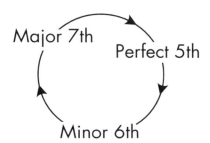

Fig. 5.11. An Interval Row. Observe that there is an interval from each interval group.

Portraying the row as a circle produces an unbroken information flow. At first, I worked from rows written in the standard linear left-to-right format. I found that the cadences of my phrases tended to end when I reached the "right" end of the line. Then I would move back to the "left" end of the line to "start up" again. With the circular format, no beginning or end of the row is visually suggested.

Here are some examples of this row in action. As in Schoenberg's tone rows, the interval row's order is essentially maintained throughout an improvisation or composition. You can use the interval going up or going down. First, we'll use a monophonic (single-note) texture.

Fig. 5.12. Interval Row: major seventh, perfect fifth, and a minor sixth, used monophonically

Next, we'll set the interval row using a *polyphonic* (contrapuntal) texture. The row's intervals unfold as the cambiata (moving line) progresses, moving against the cantus (sustained notes).

Fig. 5.13. Row Used
Polyphonically

Now for some homophonic texture—building vertical structures (chords) with each of the intervals. Observe that the first structure consists of only major seventh intervals, followed by a structure with only perfect fifths, then *only* minor sixths. Then, the row repeats, with first major sevenths, and so on. Observe how the phrase ends in a clean A major tonality, thanks to the minor sixth interval. So, if you wish things to be more tonal, you can tweak them in that direction.

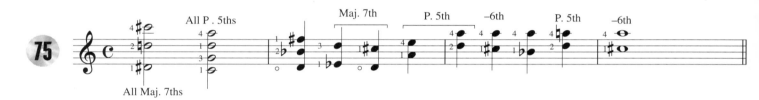

Fig. 5.14. Row Used
Homophonically

Now, for one of my favorite techniques with interval rows: quodlibet. Here, I quote "Row, Row, Row Your Boat," no pun intended, and hang the interval row on it. I added an open B string in bar 3 for color.

Interval Row with Quodlibet on "Row, Row, Row Your Boat"

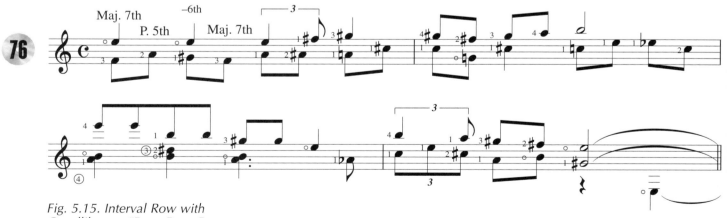

Fig. 5.15. Interval Row with
Quodlibet on "Row, Row, Row
Your Boat"

The Pandiatonic Interval Row

Interval rows can be "adjusted" to become pandiatonic, and have their intervals non-specific, quality-wise (major, minor, perfect, diminished, or augmented). Then, you can use them with a traditional scale. Let's take the row we have been using, but give it a pandiatonic attitude.

We'll choose an interval from each interval group, but now, the quality of each interval is relative to the scale used.

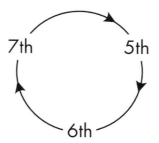

Fig. 5.16. Pandiatonic Interval Row

To illustrate this pandiatonic row, here is the same contrapuntal example used earlier. Now, it is in the A-Aeolian mode (A-natural minor). I simply removed the sharps and flats to make all (pan) the notes in the key (diatonic). As you can hear, the effect is quite different. Again, observe indications of how the interval row moves against the cantus.

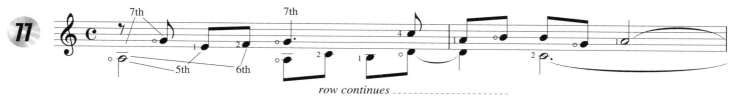

Fig. 5.17. Row used pandiaton-ically and contrapuntally

Here is another example using an interval row pandiatonically. This row is seventh, fifth, third.

Fig. 5.17. Using a Pandiatonic Row

Children's' Triptych

Here is a section of a work entitled *Children's Triptych,* in which I used the interval row of major seventh, perfect fifth, and minor sixth. As the piece progresses, I cheat a bit, which is okay! This section is called "New Surroundings," and I felt that the freshness of atonality would capture the surprise and elation of a young child in their new surroundings. (The entire work is too lengthy to include here. If you would like the entire piece, let me know!)

Children's Triptych
II. New Surroundings
For My Children Benjamin and Eugene

Jon Damian

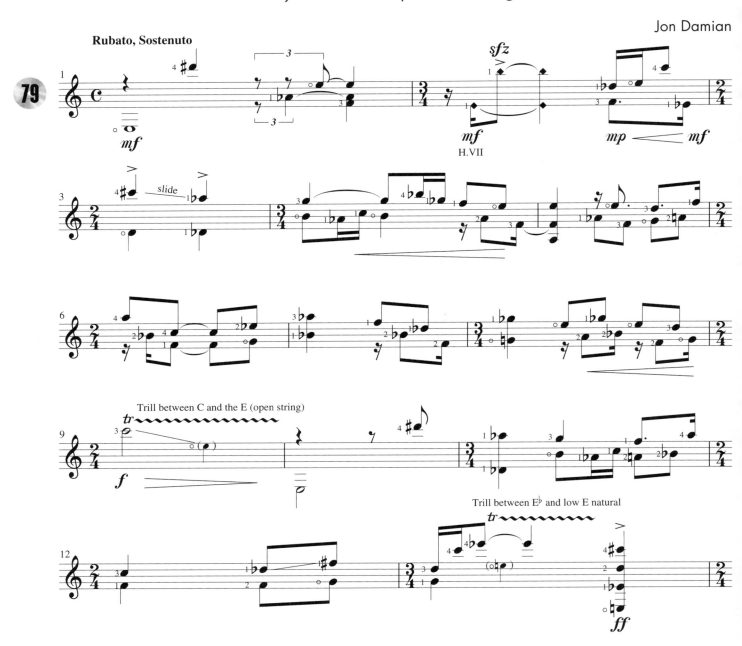

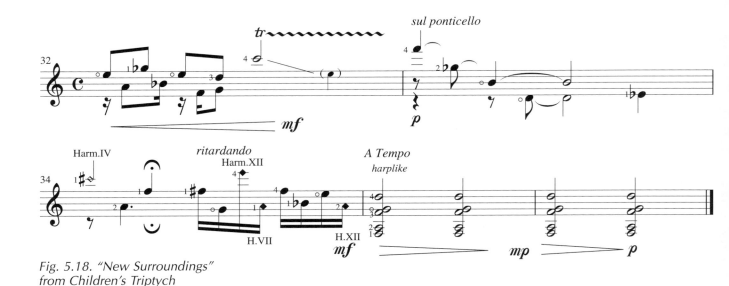

Fig. 5.18. "New Surroundings"
from Children's Triptych

Story Form, Programmatic Form

So far, we have explored a variety of form and development possibilities. We looked at standard ternary form with "Rosie." We explored using a standard progression as the form's foundation with "Falling Leaves." We opened up new ways to view the harmonic progression with the shape forms, such as Blueshape. Finally, we glimpsed at the world of atonality with tone rows and interval rows in *Children's Triptych.* Now, for a bit of story form.

Story form, or *programmatic form,* involves using a particular scenario—perhaps a play, or a poem—as the form used for a composition and/or improvisation. *The Coronation* (chapter 1) is an example of programmatic or story form. Film scores are also programmatic, as are operas, where a libretto (a story) is the source for inspiration.

I would like to close the Form chapter with a programmatic piece, conceived to work with a simple scenario, called "Mardi Gras." This piece is another conception and composition of the Creative Workshop, and it is totally improvised. The scenario is the festive atmosphere of Mardi Gras in New Orleans and the incredible layers of sound and music activity. The piece is a "comprovisation." Here is the basic score used by the four performers heard on the CD track. Consider yourself one of the players and join in!

80

 Mardi Gras

Conceived and Composed by
The Creative Workshop of Fall 1999

- It is Mardi Gras time in New Orleans. Imagine the rich layers of sound and music of Mardi Gras.

- *Before* the initial cue to begin, conceive (silently, away from the other players) a simple, repetitive, rhythmic motif—not too long—that captures one of the sound/music layers of the Mardi Gras. You will begin to play it when the initial cue is given, and then continue to play it for the beginning of the piece.

- On cue from the conductor, enter with your motif, directly with the other players.

- Maintain your *own* motif. There *should* be distinct "layers" of motifs, capturing the richness of each distinctive activity.

- Watch the conductor for cues to bring your motif up or down, dynamically. The conductor may also direct you to sing a sustained note or percussive sound, or to solo with ideas from your motif.

- When directed to sing, continue playing your motif, and sing a sustained note of your choice until you need to breathe. Then stop singing, but continue playing your motif!

- After the improvisation section, watch the conductor for cues to begin fireworking (extracting notes from) your motif.

- After the motifs have become almost totally silent, there will be a final cue. At the cue, sing one final note of your choice, without your guitar, and hold it until you need to breathe. When everyone stops singing, "Mardi Gras" is concluded.

Now, let's listen to the Creative Workshop in action with "Mardi Gras"—a good example of a story form utilized for a comprovisation. Again, this is only a portion of their 20-minute live performance! This is just one of hundreds of wonderful form ideas the Creative Workshop has developed over the years.

Chapter 6 Foundations

"Talk does not cook rice."

—Chinese Proverb

Throughout this book you have heard the mention of the Foundations chapter, so here it is! This chapter is for *all* levels. Its studies and reference materials will strengthen your basic observation abilities, enabling the effective execution of the techniques and concepts illustrated throughout this humble tome.

But why is the Foundations chapter at the *end* of the book? Having a vision of some creative goals, such as counterpoint, form, the Palette Chart, and so on, will help guide you through these following important—and at times, overwhelming—studies, and inspire you to master them.

In these Foundations, you will find scale, interval, arpeggio (chord tone), and ear studies. You'll also find reference sheets, fingerboard templates, a crossword puzzle (if you need to take a break), a scratch and sniff (just for fun!), a bibliography, and probably the most important study of all, The Incredible Time Machine Study.

Even if you feel that you have your foundations covered, the studies included here will help create a balance between your eyes *and* your ears. A regular diet of these foundation studies will help you absorb the rest of this book into your creative resources. The earlier chapters illustrated forms for the development of musical architectures. This chapter will give us the lumber from which to build.

Some Practice Points

Here are some practice points:

1. **You are *how* you practice.** The *quality* of your practice time, not the *amount* of time you practice, is what determines how efficiently your practicing develops your performance ability.

   Approach all musical examples and studies as though they were performance pieces. Include rhythmic, articulation, dynamic, and direction variation where possible to breathe musical life into everything you touch. Practice time should never be considered as different from other performance situations. It should have all the intensity and awareness you would have in any performance. "You are *how* you practice."

2. **Always begin your practicing with a period of physical and mental (ear) warm-up time.** Keep this time a consistent length. For health reasons alone, you should warm up before you practice or perform.

3. **It is important to have a feeling of completeness and musical satisfaction at the end of a practice session.** Scale, interval, arpeggio, and technical studies can seem endless unless you practice studies that have a clear form, such as a cycle or a tune's chord progression. Good

examples are Cycle Scales and Arpeggio Study, found later in this chapter. Feeling that you have completed something is especially important when working in an area that seems overwhelming in possibilities.

4. **Always end a session with a final, well played musical statement that feels good.** It could be as simple as playing one note, but play it so that the one note feels good, and that you are a part of it, like a smile.

The Studies

Let's begin by fulfilling a promise made in chapters 2 and 4. Here is a page with four fingerboard templates. The first template consists of basic note locations on the guitar fingerboard. Then, there are blank fingerboard templates for you to copy. Use them to fill in some Palette Chart seeds for melodic and harmonic development, as well as any other Foundations chapter materials.

Fingerboard Templates

These templates are for your reference. This first template consists of the note locations on the fingerboard, up to the fifteenth fret. Use this for scale, interval, and arpeggio studies.

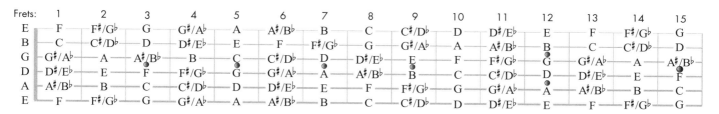

Fig. 6.1. Fingerboard Template

These blank templates are the ones I promised in chapter 4. Copy them, and fill in the Palette Chart seeds or any other studies.

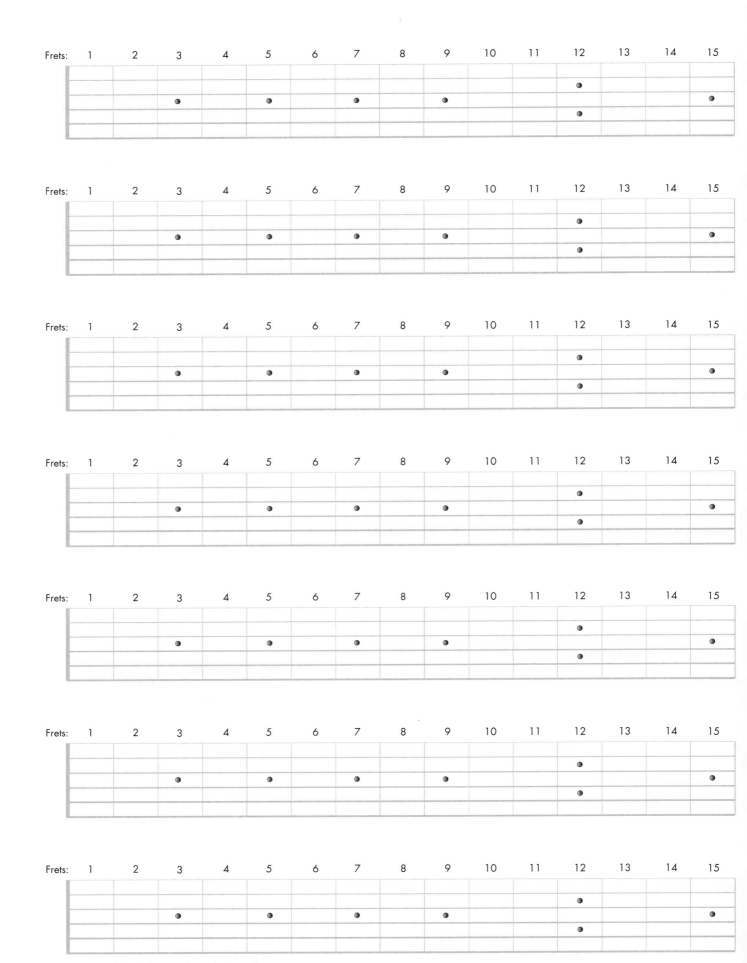

Fig. 6.2. Blank Fingerboard Templates

A Sales Pitch First

As you have probably observed, many of the concepts and ideas in this book demand a complete view of the fingerboard. By "complete," I mean being able to see and hear a particular scale's qualities, or interval(s) from that scale starting from any finger, any string. Wow! That's a lot of possibilities, because the guitar is "just crazy that way." The following studies will build a complete visual and aural foundation on the fingerboard.

I know this sounds like a paradox, but an efficient way to completely learn these fingerboard foundations is to *stay in one place* on the fingerboard. Some folks call it a "position" or an "area." Whatever you want to call it, having a location consistency when studying a particular subject, such as learning scales and intervals, is an efficient way to tap all the possibilities.

A position is determined by the fingerboard hand's second (middle) and third (ring) fingers. These fingers play only the frets on which they begin a study. A position is named by the fret preceding the middle finger. Fingers one (index) and four (pinky) occasionally stretch to play a needed note. Maintaining this basic concept will help your fingerboard hand cover all the possibilities for your eyes and ears to learn.

Remember, the last thing you want to do when playing is to stay locked in an area or position.

This sales pitch is only for these present studies. As mentioned earlier, setting limits can open up some ideas you would never have imagined!

Scales

The tonal foundation for our creative work is the scale. Intervals (for motif and seed development), counterpoint, and form concepts (such as rows) are all drawn from the humble scale. Our first look and listen at scales will be simply moving by step, *across* the fingerboard. You may find it helpful to refer to the fingerboard templates (see fig. 6.1) and the scale charts, later in this chapter.

Cycle Scales
For *Across*-the-Fingerboard Scale Visual Awareness

This first study will help you master the seeing of basic scale materials across the fingerboard. It is called Cycle Scales because it moves through *cycle V*. Cycle V refers to the interval motion *down a fifth*. The cycle is illustrated below, for your reference.

Here are the steps for Cycle Scales. Complete the cycle each time you do this study. You may wish to map out the scales on a fingerboard template.

1. **Choose any position.** (Refer to the Sales Pitch that precedes this study for details about positions/areas.)

2. **Choose any scale type.** For example, major, melodic minor, harmonic minor, and so forth.

3. **Choose a starting note on the low E string.** Make this the first scale. If you chose a B, then the first scale is a B scale of the scale type you chose in (2).

4. **Play up and down the scale.** Go from your chosen note (B) on the low E string to the same note (B) on the high E string. Then return back to the starting note (B).

5. **Play the next scale, cycle V (down a fifth) from the previous one, but from the *same starting note* (B).** If the scale you just played in (4) was B major, now play an E major scale (cycle V down from B) *but starting on B* (a B Mixolydian scale). If your starting note is not in a scale of the cycle (for example, a B is not in a B-flat major scale), then start on the note next to B—the B-flat or the C. Return to the B as your starting note when it is possible.

6. **Continue moving through the rest of the cycle to complete Cycle Scale Study.**

Again, *cycle V* or "cycle of fifths" means to move *down* a perfect fifth. Here it is starting from C.

C   F   B♭   E♭   A♭   D♭   G♭   B   E   A   D   G   C

By moving through the cycle of fifths, all the modes of the scale type you choose will be covered. Try this study in various positions and with different scale types (such as melodic and harmonic minor).

Ears One
For *Across*-the-Fingerboard Scale Awareness for Your Ears

The Ear Studies can be the toughest studies for our egos to bear. Be patient. You are doing the study perfectly if it sounds bad sometimes. It means you are listening! Gradually, things will smooth out. I promise.

The Cycle Scales Study develops scale awareness from a visual perspective. Ears One develops the same material, but this time, your ear will be working to produce the scales. Your intellect will be of little help here. Let your instinct guide you. Here are the steps for Ears One.

1. **Record a series of *random* major and minor triads.** Just use the four basic bar chords to make the tape. *Don't write anything down! Don't try to stay in one key!* This tape should be ten minutes long and filled with surprises, because it is an Ear Study! Make each bar chord last for two measures, each moving at a tempo of about quarter note equals 90. Your tape should be *at least* ten minutes in length.

2. **Sing scales against your chords.** After the tape is ready, play it back and sing scales in steady eighth notes over it. Don't think about what scales you should sing; just use your instinct. Singing helps your body experience the music. It strengthens your voice and ear. Notice your instinct at play, and how it guides your voice through the scales. Note how your voice naturally shifts a half step from a note at times to adjust to the triad on the tape. If eighth notes are too fast, try singing quarter notes.

3. **Try the study with your guitar.** After you've tried singing with the tape, try playing along with your guitar.

   - *Stay in one position area!* (See the Sales Pitch, earlier in this chapter, for details.) This will help your *hand* hear all possibilities.

   - *Play scales only.* Start on the low E string.

   - *Move in steady eighth notes.* Use quarter notes if eighths feel too fast.

   - *Don't change direction.* Keep going up the scale until you reach the high E string, then come on back down to the low E string. Continue to the end of tape. If playing the guitar to the tape is too frustrating, go back to singing for a while, to build your confidence.

Try This. As you sing with the tape, when a note doesn't sound right, your voice will naturally move chromatically to help find its way. Do the same thing when trying Ears One with your guitar. When you play that note that sounds funny, play a note chromatically (a half step) in the direction you were headed (up or down) to help your ear and hand.

Eventually, make the tape consist of more demanding harmonic sounds, and play in all the intervals. It is a good study for warming up your hands and ears. Good Luck!

The next three studies— Long Scales, Jaws, Zorro Scales, and Ears One.5— will help you see and hear scales moving *along* the fingerboard.

Long Scales
For *Along*-the-Fingerboard Scale Awareness for Your Eyes

In the Long Scales studies, the position-area strength gained from Cycle Scales will be utilized to help scale movement *along* the fingerboard. The combination of awareness gained from Cycle Scales and Long Scales will enable you to achieve full fingerboard accessibility and tonal mobility. This tonal mobility increases access to ideas that the position areas don't. It is also helpful for using many of the techniques we have been exploring, such as the Palette Chart studies.

First, here is a simple study to help your hand adapt to motion along the fingerboard. It is called Jaws Study.

Take a break here and

try the crossword

puzzle at the end of

this chapter!

Jaws Study

The name of this study comes from the sound of the first few examples given below. The first example sounds something like the theme from the classic white shark thriller. These short studies are not designed to frighten you, but to help the fingerboard hand feel more at home moving *along* the fingerboard. Playing along the fingerboard not only increases your mobility, but also facilitates seeing and playing scale structures found *along* the strings. This technique is very important for using scale information, such as the 3-note melodic motifs and harmonic seeds from the Palette Chart.

The studies will develop your ability to shift efficiently between positions. To move up the fingerboard efficiently, after playing with the third or fourth finger in the old position, start the new higher position with your first or second fingers on the higher fret (see fig. 6.3). The studies also develop the movement of your first (or sometimes second) finger *down* to your third or fourth finger to complete a position shift *down* the fingerboard.

Play the examples slowly at first. Eventually, try them with your eyes closed. This will help you feel the shifts more, since you can't watch your fingerboard hand.

Remember, a circled number indicates a string, and a plain number, the fingering.

Repeat each bar on the low E string several times with each fingering variation. Use the fingerings marked! When you can play it easily, try it with your eyes closed.

JaWs Study

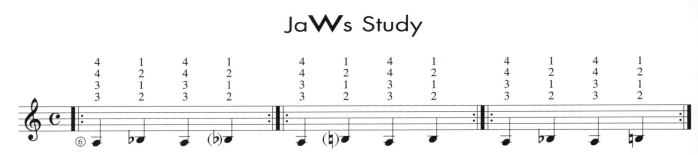

Fig. 6.3. Jaws Notes

Zorro Scales

Do you remember Zorro, the famous swordsman who left his famous mark of the Z everywhere, mostly on his enemies' chests? In Zorro Scales, you will make the famous mark of Zorro on the fingerboard!

Illustrated below, using some of the finger shifts learned in Jaws Study, is a simple F major scale. It moves up and along the low E string, then down and along to the bottom of the A string, then up and along to the top of the D string, and so forth, producing this zigzag Zorro-like shape through the fingerboard! The shifts indicated are just one possibility. Explore others as well. Eventually, try this study in all keys and scale types and with intervals and 3- and 4-note structures. Zorro Study is an efficient study for learning to see basic scale materials *along* the fingerboard. This foundation will help you build the structures used in the Palette Chart.

Zorro Scales
In F Major

Fig. 6.4. Zorro Scales

Ears One.5
For *Along*-the-Fingerboard Scale Awareness for Your Ears

Ears One.5 is similar to Ears One except that instead of staying in a position area, for this study, you will move Zorro fashion *along* the strings, accompanied by your tape. (Refer to Ears One, earlier in this chapter, for how to make and use the tape.) The only difference in Ears One.5 is that your ears guide you *along* the strings of the fingerboard, instead of *across* the fingerboard, as in Ears One.

Scale Reference Charts

Here are some scale-reference charts for study. The first is a cross-reference chart for all the modes of the major scales.

The second chart is another look at the modes of major. On the left side are the modes from the C major scale. On the right is a listing of all modes of major from a common starting note, C.

The third chart consists of the modes of the melodic minor scale on the left and the modes of the harmonic minor scale on the right. From this sheet, build your own cross-reference charts for the melodic minor and harmonic minor modes.

The fourth chart is a look at the symmetrically built scales: the chromatic scale, the diminished scale, and the whole-tone scale.

Finally, many of these modes are put to work with the Chord Scale Vamps study, which follows the scale reference charts. In all charts, enharmonic equivalents are used for clarity.

Modes of Major Cross-Reference Chart

Mode		Ionian	Dorian	Phrygian	Lydian	Mixolydian	Aeolian	Locrian
ROOTS:	C	C D E F G A B	C D E♭ F G A B♭	C D♭ E♭ F G A♭ B♭	C D E F♯ G A B	C D E F G A B♭	C D E♭ F G A♭ B♭	C D♭ E♭ F G♭ A♭ B♭
	C♯	C♯ D♯ F F♯ G♯ A♯ B♯	C♯ D♯ E F♯ G♯ A♯ B	C♯ D E F♯ G♯ A B	C♯ D♯ F G G♯ A♯ C	C♯ D♯ E♯ F♯ G♯ A♯ B	C♯ D♯ E F♯ G♯ A B	C♯ D E F♯ G A B
	D♭	D♭ E♭ F G♭ A♭ B♭ C	D♭ E♭ F♭ G♭ A♭ B♭ B	D♭ D E G♭ A♭ A B	D♭ E♭ F G A♭ B♭ C	D♭ E♭ F G♭ A♭ B♭ B	D♭ E♭ E G♭ A♭ A B	D♭ D E G♭ G A B
	D	D E F♯ G A B C♯	D E F G A B C	D E♭ F G A B♭ C	D E F♯ G♯ A B C♯	D E F♯ G A B C	D E F♯ G A B♭ C	D E♭ F G A♭ B♭ C
	E♭	E♭ F G A♭ B♭ C D	E♭ F G♭ A♭ B♭ C D♭	E♭ E G♭ A♭ B♭ B D♭	E♭ F G A B♭ C D	E♭ F G A♭ B♭ C D♭	E♭ F G♭ A♭ B♭ B D♭	E♭ E G♭ A♭ A B D♭
	E	E F♯ G♯ A B C♯ D♯	E F♯ G A B C♯ D	E F G A B C D	E F♯ G♯ A♯ B C♯ D♯	E F♯ G♯ A B C♯ D	E F♯ G A B C D	E F G A B♭ C D
	F	F G A B♭ C D E	F G A♭ B♭ C D E♭	F G♭ A♭ B♭ C D♭ E♭	F G A B C D E	F G A B♭ C D E♭	F G A♭ B♭ C D♭ E♭	F G♭ A♭ B♭ B D♭ E♭
	F♯	F♯ G♯ A♯ B C♯ D♯ E♯	F♯ G♯ A B C♯ D♯ E	F♯ G A B C♯ D E	F♯ G♯ A♯ C C♯ D♯ F	F♯ G♯ A♯ B C♯ D♯ E	F♯ G♯ A B C♯ D E	F♯ G A B C D E
	G♭	G♭ A♭ B♭ C♭ D♭ E♭ F	G♭ A♭ B C♭ D♭ E♭ E	G♭ G A B D♭ D E	G♭ A♭ B♭ C D♭ E♭ F	G♭ A♭ B♭ B D♭ E♭ E	G♭ A♭ A B D♭ D E	G♭ G A B C D E
	G	G A B C D E F♯	G A B♭ C D E F	G A♭ B♭ C D E♭ F	G A B C♯ D E F♯	G A B C D E F	G A B♭ C D E♭ F	G A♭ B♭ C D♭ E♭ F
	A♭	A♭ B♭ C D♭ E♭ F G	A♭ B♭ C♭ D♭ E♭ F G♭	A♭ A B D♭ E♭ E G♭	A♭ B♭ C D E♭ F G	A♭ B♭ C D♭ E♭ F G♭	A♭ B♭ B D♭ E♭ E G♭	A♭ A B D♭ D E G♭
	A	A B C♯ D E F♯ G♯	A B C D E F♯ G	A B♭ C D E F G	A B C♯ D♯ E F♯ G♯	A B C♯ D E F♯ G	A B C D E F G	A B♭ C D E F G
	B♭	B♭ C D E♭ F G A	B♭ C D♭ E♭ F G A♭	B♭ B D♭ E♭ F G♭ A♭	B♭ C D E F G A	B♭ C D E♭ F G A♭	B♭ C D♭ E♭ F G♭ A♭	B♭ B D♭ E♭ E G♭ A♭
	B	B C♯ D♯ E F♯ G♯ A♯	B C♯ D E F♯ G♯ A	B C D E F♯ G A	B C♯ D♯ E♯ F♯ G♯ A♯	B C♯ D♯ E F♯ G♯ A	B C♯ D E F♯ G A	B C D E F G A

Fig. 6.5. Modes of Major Cross-Reference Chart

Modes of Major

As seen from Diatonic Degrees | **As seen from Consistent Root**

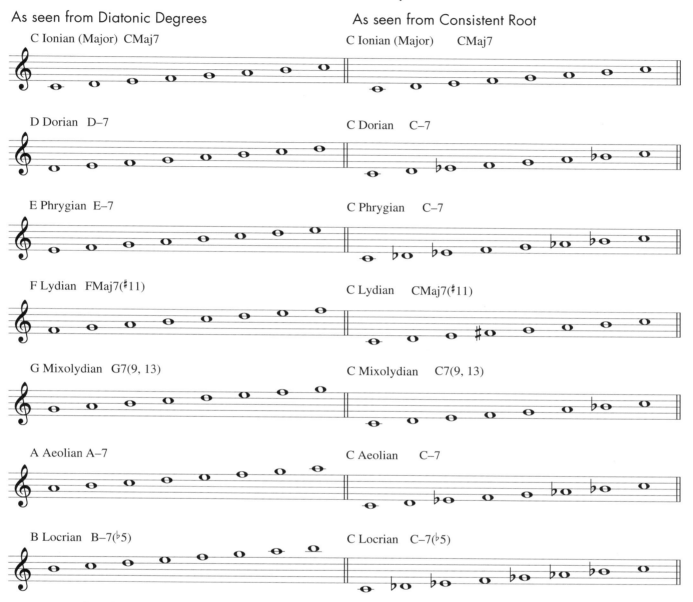

C Ionian (Major) CMaj7 — C Ionian (Major) CMaj7

D Dorian D–7 — C Dorian C–7

E Phrygian E–7 — C Phrygian C–7

F Lydian FMaj7(♯11) — C Lydian CMaj7(♯11)

G Mixolydian G7(9, 13) — C Mixolydian C7(9, 13)

A Aeolian A–7 — C Aeolian C–7

B Locrian B–7(♭5) — C Locrian C–7(♭5)

*Fig. 6.6. Modes of Major and All
Modes Beginning on C*

Here are the modes of the C melodic minor and C harmonic minor scales.
The more commonly used modes are named in bold type.

Modes of Melodic Minor   Modes of Harmonic Minor
Bold Face designates more commonly used scale

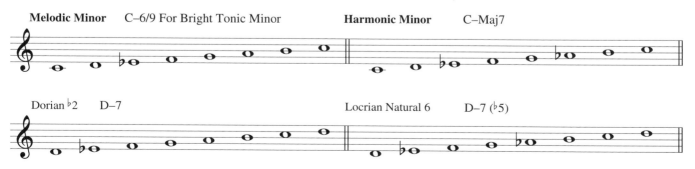

Melodic Minor C–6/9 For Bright Tonic Minor — **Harmonic Minor** C–Maj7

Dorian ♭2 D–7 — Locrian Natural 6 D–7 (♭5)

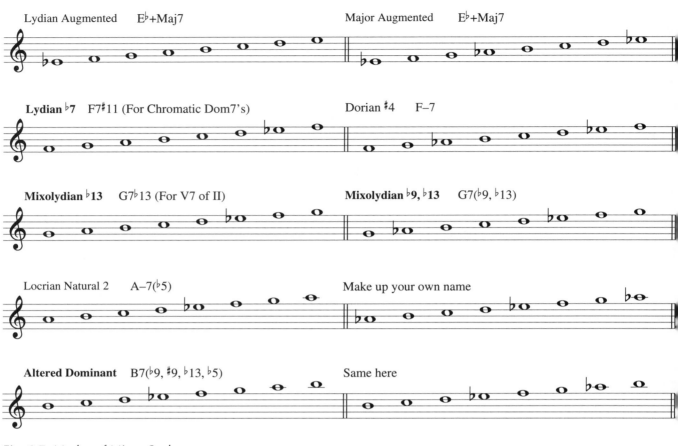

Fig. 6.7. Modes of Minor Scales

Symmetric Scales

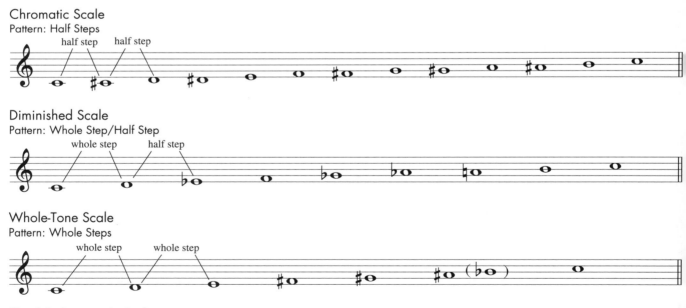

Fig. 6.8. Symmetric Scales

Chord Scale Vamps

Let's put all this scale info to work. The following *vamps* (short, repeated progressions) use various chord-scales. Above each chord symbol is the chord's tonal function, and below it is a suggested scale. The indicated functions and scales are the simplest choices, but you may have a different interpretation.

Make a simple tape of these vamps, repeating each as often as you like. Then improvise along with the tape, using the suggested scales (or your own).

Vamp No. 1

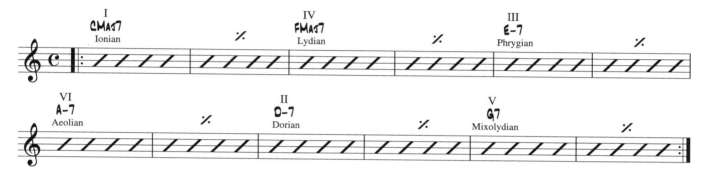

Vamp No. 2

Lydian major is used on ♭IIMaj7, ♭IIIMaj7, ♭VIMaj7, and ♭VIIMaj7.

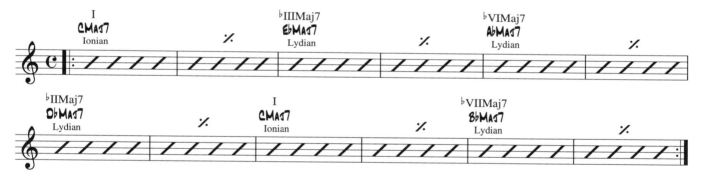

Vamp No. 3

Mixolydian is used here for secondary dominant 7 chords moving to major chords (V/IV and V/V).

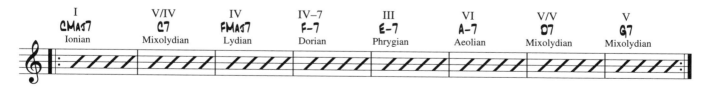

Vamp No. 4

On V7 chords moving to a minor chord, use the mode found from the fifth degree of the harmonic minor scale of the target minor chord. This mode is called Mixolydian ♭9♭13.

Vamp No. 5

Here is the Mixolydian ♭9♭13 scale in use with secondary dominant 7 chords moving to minor chords (V/II, VI/III, and V/VI).

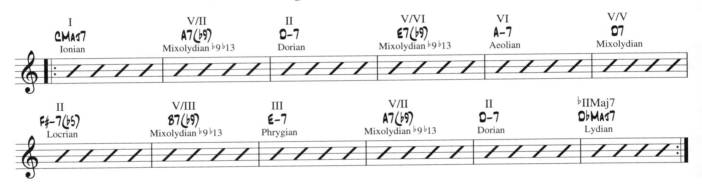

Vamp No. 6

Here is the Mixolydian ♭9♭13 scale used on some diminished 7 chords, which are functioning as secondary dominant 7 chords, moving to minor chords.

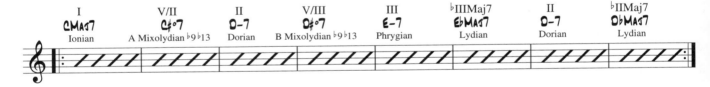

Vamp No. 7

The melodic minor scale can be used with I–6 and IV–6.

Vamp No. 8

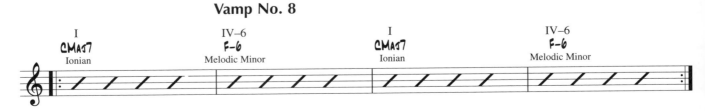

Vamp No. 9

The mode of melodic minor, from the fourth degree (the Lydian ♭7 scale) is used on IV dominant 7 chords, and chromatically moving dominant 7 chords, which are substitute V7 chords.

Vamp No. 10

The mode of melodic minor from the seventh degree, the altered scale, can be used on V7 chords.

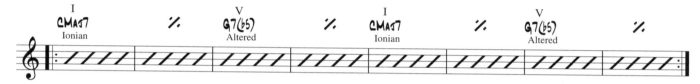

Vamp No. 11

The diminished scale can be used for diminished chords and for V7 chords starting from the 3, 5, 7, or ♭9 degree of the dominant 7 chord.

Vamp No. 12

The whole-tone scale is used here on a V7 chord with an augmented fifth degree.

Fig. 6.9. Chord Scale Vamps

This section has been a basic look at scales. There are more possibilities. Scales are merely tonal guides to help the ear and eyes, and to open new areas that the ear hasn't learned about yet. Eventually, the ear will make its own decisions.

Have fun with these vamps. They are like an aerobics workout, and will be as musical as you make them.

Interval Studies

Our first interval study was introduced back in chapter 2, with Pitch Motif Studies, where we worked diatonic intervals through the scales.

In Ears 2, we will work on hearing and singing these intervals. The Interval Cross-Reference chart is included for your reference.

Ears Two

1. **Choose a position area for study.** (See the position rap earlier in this chapter.)

2. **Choose an interval and direction for study.** For example, you might choose minor thirds ascending.

3. **Play a note in your position chosen in (1), and from this note, *sing* the note based on your interval and direction chosen in (2).** Continue playing the first note and then creating harmony with your voice. Feel the interval quality in your throat and chest as you sing with the note. Re-attack the fingered note if needed.

4. **Now *play* the chosen interval/direction (minor third ascending) on your guitar.** If you were singing the correct note, good. If not, play the starting note again and try singing again with your instrument's help.

5. **Continue.** Play another note and continue as above. Give all fingerboard-hand fingers and all strings a chance at the starting note! This will help you learn to see and hear all fingering possibilities for the intervals.

Eventually, identification of intervals by ear will become as easy as color identification is to your eyes. Picturing a hand-shape on the fingerboard will trigger a sound in your imagination, as well.

Interval Cross-Reference Chart

	−2	Maj2	−3	Maj3	P4	♯4	Dim 5	P5	♯5	−6	Maj6	♭7	Maj7
C	D♭	D	E♭	E	F	F♯	G♭	G	G♯	A♭	A	B♭	B
C♯	D	D♯	E	E♯	F♯	G	G	G♯	A	A	A♯	B	B♯
D♭	D	E♭	E	F	G♭	G	G	A♭	A	A	B♭	C♭	C
D	E♭	E	F	F♯	G	G♯	A♭	A	A♯	B♭	B	C	C♯
D♯	E	E♯	F♯	G	G♯	A	A	A♯	B	B	B♯	C♯	D
E♭	E	F	G♭	G	A♭	A	A	B♭	B	C♭	C	D♭	D
E	F	F♯	G	G♯	A	A♯	B♭	B	B♯	C	C♯	D	D♯
F	G♭	G	A♭	A	B♭	B	C♭	C	C♯	D♭	D	E♭	E
F♯	G	G♯	A	A♯	B	B♯	C	C♯	D	D	D♯	E	E♯
G♭	G	A♭	A	B♭	C♭	B♯	C	D♭	D	D	E♭	E	F
G	G♯	A	B♭	B	C	C♯	D♭	D	D♯	E♭	E	F	F♯
G♯	A	A♯	B	B♯	C♯	D	D	D♯	E	E	E♯	F♯	F
A♭	A	B♭	C♭	C	D♭	D	D	E♭	E	F♭	F	G♭	G
A	B♭	B	C	C♯	D	D♯	E♭	E	E♯	F	F♯	G	G♯
A♯	B	B♯	C♯	D	D♯	E	E	E♯	F♯	F♯	G	G♯	A
B♭	C♭	C	D♭	D	E♭	E	F♭	F	F♯	G♭	G	A♭	A
B	C	C♯	D	D♯	E	E♯	F	F♯	G	G	G♯	A	A♯

Fig. 6.10. Interval Cross-Reference Chart. Enharmonic equivalents are used for clarity.

The left column contains the intervals' bottom notes. The top row contains the interval qualities. Use it like a mileage chart! For example, if you want a major 7 interval above D, find the desired bottom note (in this case D) in the left column, then move across the top row to find the major 7 interval quality. At their intersection, you have your destination!

Take another break here and try the crossword puzzle at the end of this chapter!

Arpeggio Study

Arpeggios are valuable resources for composition and improvisation. They consist of the *simplest resting notes* relative to a harmony or chord symbol. Learning these resting points is a strong resource for mainstream improvisation, as well as extended improvisational explorations (such as Counterpoint from Chord Symbols in chapter 3, and the Pitch Motif Studies in chapter 2).

Arpeggio Study focuses on developing your ability to learn all arpeggio possibilities. Why learn them at all? Because *tonal gravity*—the tendency of notes to return to rest—exists in nature, whether you like it or not. Being able to *hear* or at least *see* these tendencies is as critical as a juggler needing to learn about the Earth's physical gravity. For your reference, I include also the Chord Tones (Arpeggios) Cross-Reference Chart.

1. **Choose a chord progression for study.**

2. **Choose a position area (see the Sales Pitch, earlier in this chapter, for details).**

3. **Play the full-position arpeggio of each chord.** Go from the lowest possible in-position chord tone on the low E string to the highest chord tone (stay in position) on the high E string. Then descend back down to the low E string. Stay in position.

Chord Tones Reference Chart

	C	C♯/D♭	D	E♭	E	F	F♯/G♭	G	A♭	A	B♭	B
Maj. Triad	C E G	C♯ E♯ G♯	D F♯ A	E♭ G B♭	E G♯ B	F A C	F♯ A♯ C♯	G B D	A♭ C E♭	A C♯ E	B♭ D F	B D♯ F♯
R, Maj.3, P.5		D♭ F A♭					G♭ B♭ D♭					
Min. Triad	C E♭ G	C♯ E G♯	D F A	E♭ G♭ B♭	E G B	F A♭ C	F♯ A C♯	G B♭ D	A♭ B E♭	A C E	B♭ D♭ F	B D F♯
R, −3, P.5		D♭ E A♭					G♭ A D♭					
Dim. Triad	C E♭ G♭	C♯ E G	D F A♭	E♭ G♭ A	E G B♭	F A♭ C♭	F♯ A C	G B♭ D♭	A♭ B D	A C E♭	B♭ D♭ F♭	B D F
R, −3, ♭5		D♭ F♭ G					G♭ A C					
Aug. Triad	C E G♯	C♯ E♯ A	D F♯ A♯	E♭ G B	E G♯ B♯	F A C♯	F♯ A♯ D	G B D♯	A♭ C E	A C♯ E♯	B♭ D F♯	B D♯ G
R, Maj.3, ♯5		D♭ F A					G♭ B♭ D					
Major 7	C E G B	C♯ E♯ G♯ C	D F♯ A C♯	E♭ G B♭ D	E G♯ B D♯	F A C E	F♯ A♯ C♯ E♯	G B D F♯	A♭ C E♭ G	A C♯ E G♯	B♭ D F A	B D♯ F♯ A♯
R, Maj.3, P.5, Maj.7		D♭ F A♭ C					G♭ B♭ D♭ F					
Dom. 7	C E G B♭	C♯ E♯ G♯ B	D F♯ A C	E♭ G B♭ D♭	E G♯ B D	F A C E♭	F♯ A♯ C♯ E	G B D F	A♭ C E♭ G♭	A C♯ E G	B♭ D F A♭	B D♯ F♯ A
R, Maj.3, P.5, ♭7		D♭ F A♭ C♭					G♭ B♭ D♭ F♭					
Min. 7	C E♭ G B♭	C♯ E G♯ B	D F A C	E♭ G♭ B♭ D♭	E G B D	F A♭ C E♭	F♯ A C♯ E	G B♭ D F	A♭ C♭ E♭ G♭	A C E G	B♭ D♭ F A♭	B D F♯ A
R, −3, P.5, ♭7		D♭ F♭ A♭ B					G♭ A D♭ F♭					
Min. 7 (♭5)	C E♭ G♭ B♭	C♯ E G B	D F A♭ C	E♭ G♭ A D♭	E G B♭ D	F A♭ B E♭	F♯ A C E	G B♭ D♭ F	A♭ B D G♭	A C E♭ G	B♭ D♭ F♭ A♭	B D F A
R, −3, ♭5, ♭7		D♭ F♭ G B					G♭ A C E					
Min. 6	C E♭ G A	C♯ E G♯ A♯	D F A B	E♭ G♭ B♭ C	E G B C♯	F A♭ C D	F♯ A C♯ D♯	G B♭ D E	A♭ C♭ E♭ F	A C E F♯	B♭ D♭ F G	B D F♯ G♯
R, −3, P.5, Maj.6		D♭ F♭ A♭ B♭					G♭ A D♭ E♭					
Dim. 7	C E♭ G♭ A	C♯ E G B♭	D F A♭ B	E♭ G♭ A C	E G B♭ D♭	F A♭ B D	F♯ A C E♭	G B♭ D♭ E	A♭ C♭ D F	A C E♭ G♭	B♭ D♭ F♭ G	B D F A♭
R, −3, ♭5, Dim.7		D♭ E G B♭					G♭ A C E♭					
Dom. 7♯5	C E G♯ B♭	C♯ E♯ A B	D F♯ A♯ C	E♭ G B D♭	E G♯ C D	F A C♯ E♭	F♯ A♯ D E	G B D♯ F	A♭ C E G♭	A C♯ E♯ G	B♭ D F♯ A♭	B D♯ G A
R, Maj.3, ♯5, ♭7		D♭ F A B					G♭ B♭ D E					
Dom. 7♭5	C E G♭ B♭	C♯ E♯ G B	D F♯ A♭ C	E♭ G A D♭	E G♯ B♭ D	F A C♭ E♭	F♯ A♯ C E	G B D♭ F	A♭ C D G♭	A C♯ E♭ G	B♭ D F♭ A♭	B D♯ F A
R, Maj.3, ♭5, ♭7		D♭ F G B					G♭ B♭ C F♭					

Fig. 6.11. Chord Tones Reference Chart.

In the Chord Tone Reference Chart (fig. 6.9), you can quickly look up the notes in an arpeggio. The left column contains arpeggio or chord qualities, and the top row contains root of desired arpeggio or chord. For example, if you want to get D major 7, find the root D in top row, and then move down vertically to row with desired quality (major 7) in the left column. Then, you have the notes!

More Ears!

Here is one last Ear Study. I actually have close to 58 Ear Studies! The only thing I can tell you about Ears 57.5 is that it's dangerous and *very* expensive! The cost for the helicopter alone would put a serious dent in your wallet!

Identifying sounds is more than hearing a sound and calling it a name. Try to let sounds trigger a visual image for you. This may help you recognize it later. Or imagine a particular aroma from a sound. Seriously, it can work! Using these other imagination senses of eyes and nose can really add to your ear's abilities.

In fact (I've been waiting for the whole book to do this!!!), here is a Scratch and Sniff (it's really a fake one, but please humor me). It's a Scratch and Sniff of a CMaj7(♯11) chord symbol. Scratch the symbol, and imagine: What aroma does it have?

(It's really a fake)

Fig. 6.12. Scratch and Sniff

Ears Three: *For general identification of harmonic sounds*

The following study will help you recognize harmonic sounds.

1. **Choose a harmonic sound you wish to study.** Is it 2-note intervals? Basic chords? Seeds from the Palette Chart?

2. **Make a list of the sound qualities you'll use.** Let's say that you chose "basic chords" in (1). Use some or all of the chord qualities listed on the Arpeggio/Chord Cross-Reference Chart (see fig. 6.9).

3. **Get ready to record.** Now, you will begin to create a tape of chords. You will record a 30-minute tape.

4. **Play one of the chord types, based on a root of your choice.** For example, D minor 7. Set the metronome at about 90 beats per minute, and begin recording. Play your chord for eight beats (two measures of 4/4).

5. **Say the chord's name.** After the first bar, as you begin playing the second bar, say the name of the chord you are playing.

6. **Repeat.** Reference your list from (2) as you make the tape, randomly choosing new chord qualities. Play each chord for two bars. Choose another quality of chord and root note for two bars, say, an augmented B-flat triad. Again, at the beginning of the second bar, say the chord name.

7. **Finish the tape.** Continue in this manner, randomly choosing chord types and roots, until a full 30 minutes has elapsed. Remember, each harmonic sound lasts eight beats, and the second measure begins with your voice stating the chord's name and quality. The tape should consist of a good mixture of chord types, and your voice identifying which is which.

8. **Listen.** Now, play the tape back and try guessing the chord type you hear in the first four beats before your voice identifies the structure. It is important that you can observe the chord's sound first, rather than your voice stating what's coming. As mentioned above, let the sound trigger a visual image or an aroma that you can relate to it. If you need to make your lists shorter, go right ahead.

Try various types of lists. Use palette seeds, intervals, or any other sounds.

The Incredible Time Machine Study

Our growth and development as musicians is seldom as consistent as we would like. Some days, we ride the crest of our development cycle, with our confidence strong in our abilities. Other days, the downside makes us feel like we are not making any progress at all. I can safely say that I've been riding this crazy roller coaster of development longer than most of you, and have drawn some conclusions that may help smooth out the rest of your ride a bit. During what used to be my down days, I'd get depressed, beef about things, and gradually wait until the cycle turned for the better. It began to get tiring.

I began to notice that just before a down cycle hit, a significant musical trauma hit me first. In chapter 1, I mentioned the conductor squawking that I was too loud. A simple request, but crushing for my tender ego. But I did learn to respect dynamic markings a whole lot better, after that.

Another time, I was performing with a dear friend, D. Sharpe. After finishing a set, he asked me if I was listening to him at all. I lied, and said sure, but realized that I was so self-involved that I wasn't aware of the great ideas he was trying to feed me. Again, my ego was crushed, but my ensemble awareness sure took a turn for the better.

My greatest moments of musical enlightenment have occurred during many "sensitive" moments like these. I have come to realize that when that downside occurs, it is actually a positive sign that a light just went on, enabling me to view the next subject in my developmental progression more clearly. It simply means that my observation of a particular musical area has strengthened, enabling me to take another step forward.

It took me a while to feel more positive about those downside days, but now, that cycle isn't quite as topsy-turvy as it used to be. In fact, if I didn't have those downsides, I'd probably feel like a light went out, since now I realize that downward swing is just giving me momentum to pop up to the next plateau.

Here's a simple fun thing to try if you are feeling overwhelmed and in one of those slumps. It's called "The Incredible Time Machine Study."

 # The Incredible Time Machine Study

Did you ever feel like going back in time for some crazy reason? Well, as guitar players, we're lucky, because we can sort of do it.

Check this out. Let's say you hit one of those days when you feel like your progress as a player has hit a brick wall. Take your guitar and simply reverse the whole kit 'n caboodle. You are now holding the guitar so that your normal fingerboard hand is holding the pick and your other hand is fingering the notes and chords. The pegboard is now facing east instead of west. Got it? Feels strange? Of course, because this is a lot how it felt that first day you picked up this beast! You have gone back several years in time. Well, kinda….

Now, let's go to work. Play something that has become pretty instinctive for you, by now. Try a pentatonic scale. If you were holding your guitar regularly, this pentatonic scale would be something you could play while watching a movie and eating popcorn! But now, since you've taken a step back in time, your instinct is fairly useless. This simple pentatonic scale takes some real determination and intellect to figure out.

Next, try a simple chord progression. Try playing an F bar chord! Wow! And ouch!! I can still remember the shock of trying my first bar chord. In time-machine mode, it's tough, but in regular mode we play these chords without a second thought.

It's simply because you've come a long way, baby! Many hours of practice, performance, hard work, determination, and intellectual ability have helped you make a technique become an instinctive ability. Some days, it's difficult to see progress, because you are with yourself all the time. It's tough to step back and gauge progress when you are right up close to things. But when you take this simple step backwards in time, you not only appreciate the progress you've made, but can also feel better about all the new intellectual techniques being thrown at you.

Eventually, with your continued hard work, these new techniques will also become part of your musical instinct.

The Guitarist's Guide Crossword Puzzle Challenge

Most answers are somewhere in this book.

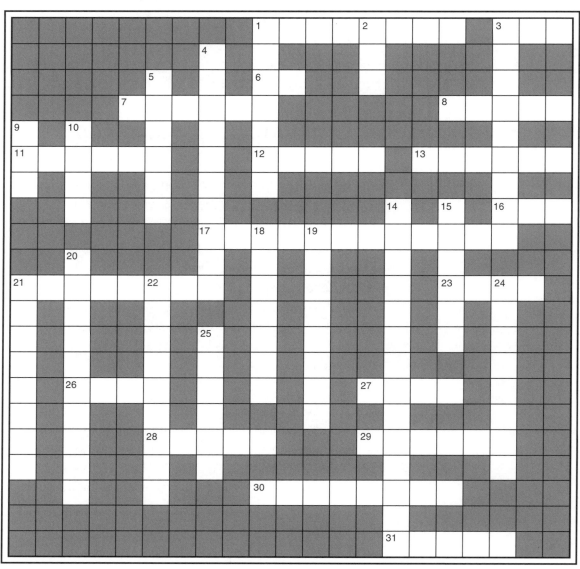

ACROSS

1. Repetition and _____
3. To like in jazz
6. What goes down must go____
7. Sustained part of counterpoint
8. What sprouts from Palette Chart
11. No key
12. A study
13. Your ax
16. Guitar's relative
17. Musical speech
21. A French form
23. Plectrum
26. To play perfectly
27. A bit of music
28. A dancer's support
29. Horizontal
30. Soft, softer
31. Idea

DOWN

1. As in grapes
2. Progression of events
3. A sound dimension
4. Backwards
5. Salivating dogs
9. Measure
10. What goes _____ must go up
14. All notes in key equal
15. Opposite of compound
18. Monophonic, Polyphonic
19. Two or more simple lines
20. Tone rows founder
21. Moving counterpoint
22. Pickpocket technique
24. Opposite motion
25. Turn upside down

Bye-Bop Quiz Answers from Chapter 2
"Confirmation" and "Ornithology"

Coda

If you are reading this, that's a good sign. You made it this far in the book, which obviously made it to press, to your home, and most importantly, hopefully, to becoming one of the inspirations in your musical journey, with this instrument of endless possibilities. I would love to meet you and learn from you, so call, write, or e-mail me with your ideas. You be the cambiata, and I'll be the cantus, then we'll switch!

It would be fun to have a collection of compositions and/or improvisations penned by my readers. I could call it *Reflections for the Guitar.* Please send me any reflections you may have that were inspired by this book. Hopefully, a curious collection of writings will be possible.

Good luck, and thanks for being the most important part of this book. "Does a falling tree make a sound if there is no one there to hear it?" It is difficult to say, but I'm sure that they appreciate being heard, so thank you for listening.

Jon Damian

c/o Berklee College of Music
1140 Boylston Street, Box 192
Boston, MA 02215
jdamian@berklee.edu

Bibliography

American Heritage Dictionary, Third Edition. Boston: Houghton-Mifflin, 1992.

Bailey, Derek. *Improvisation: Its Nature and Practice In Music.* New York: Da Capo, 2000.

Doczi, Gyorgy. *The Power of Limits.* Boston: Shambhala Press, 1994.

Fux, Johann Joseph. *Gradus Ad Parnassum.* Compiled by Alfred Mann. New York: W.W. Norton & Norton, 1971.

Gallwey, Timothy and Barry Green. *The Inner Game of Music.* Garden City, NY: Anchor Press/Doubleday, 1986.

Gold, Robert S. *A Jazz Lexicon.* New York: Alfred A. Knopf, 1957.

Goodrick, Mick. *The Advancing Guitarist.* New York: Hal Leonard Publishing Corp., 1987.

Hall, Jim. *Exploring Jazz Guitar.* Milwaukee: Hal Leonard Corporation, 1991.

Leavitt, William G. *A Modern Method for Guitar.* Boston: Berklee Press, 2000.

Murchie, Guy. *The Music of the Spheres.* New York: Dover, 1967.

Persechetti, Vincent. *Twentieth-Century Harmony.* New York: W.W. Norton & Norton, 1961.

Prosser, Steve. *Essential Ear Training for Musicians.* Boston: Berklee Press, 2000.

Roch, Pascual. *A Modern Method for the Guitar: The School of Francisco Tarrega.* New York: G.W. Schirmer, 1924.

Rufer, Joseph. *Composition with Twelve Tone.* Westport, CT: Greewood Press, 1974.

Sor, Fernando. *Method for the Spanish Guitar.* Translated into English by A. Merrick. New York: Da Capo Press, 1971 (first published in 1830).

Toch, Ernst. *The Shaping Forces in Music.* New York: Dover, 1977.

For Sight Reading Study

Bartók, Bela. *44 Violin Duets Vols. I and II.* New York: Boosey and Hawkes, 1939.

Bona, Pasquale. *Rhythmic Articulation.* New York: Calmus, 1989.

Edlund, Lars. *Modus Novus.* Stockholm: AB Nordisca Musikförlaget, 1964.

Kamien, Roger. *The Norton Scores: An Anthology for Listening.* New York: W. W. Norton & Co., 1990.

Koehler, Ernesto. *40 Progressive Duets Opus 55.* New York: Carl Fischer, 1947.

Leavitt, William G. *Melodic Rhythms.* Boston: Berklee Press, 2000.

Nelson, Oliver. *Patterns For Improvisation.* Los Angeles: Noslen Press, 1966.

Prosser, Steve. *Intervallic Training for Musicians.* Boston: Sol Ra Press, 1990.

Voisin, Roger. *Develop Sight Reading Vols. I & II.* New York, Charles Colin, 1972.

Jon Damian Biography

Jon Damian's work as a performer, composer, lecturer, and clinician has taken him to five continents. His varied performances range from Bill Frisell to Luciano Pavarotti, and from the Boston Symphony Orchestra under Seiji Ozawa to the Boston Pops under John Williams with Johnny Cash. He has performed with Jaki Byard, Leonard Bernstein, Howard McGhee, Jimmy Giuffre, Sheila Jordan, Ricky Ford, Joanne Brackeen, Don Byron, Bobby Watson, Rosemary Clooney, and Linda Rondstadt. He is professor of guitar at Berklee College of Music, and his students have included Bill Frisell, Mark Whitfield, Kurt Rosenwinkel, Leni Stern, and Wayne Krantz. His new CD, *Dedications: Faces and Places*, with Bill Frisell, features the rubbertellie—an instrument of his own invention.

THE BEST OF BERKLEE PRESS

GUITAR

Guitar Books by William Leavitt

Berklee Basic Guitar - Phase 1
0-634-01333-5 Book $7.95

Berklee Basic Guitar - Phase 2
0-7935-5526-4 Book $7.95

Classical Studies for Pick-Style Guitar
0-634-01339-4 Book $9.95

A Modern Method for Guitar
Volume 1: Beginner
0-87639-013-0 Book/CD $22.95

0-87639-014-9 Book $14.95

Volume 2: Intermediate
0-87639-016-5 Book/CD $22.95

0-87639-015-7 Book $14.95

Volume 3: Advanced
0-87639-017-3 Book $14.95

1-2-3 Complete
0-87639-011-4 Book $29.95

Melodic Rhythms for Guitar
0-634-01332-7 Book $14.95

Reading Studies for Guitar
0-634-01335-1 Book $14.95

Advanced Reading Studies for Guitar
0-634-01337-8 Book $14.95

Jim Kelly Guitar Workshop Series
Jim Kelly's Guitar Workshop
0-7935-8572-4 Book/CD $14.95

0-634-00865-X DVD $29.95
More Guitar Workshop
0-7935-9454-4 Book/CD $14.95
0-634-00648-7 VHS $19.95

BASS

The Bass Player's Handbook
by Greg Mooter
0-634-02300-4 Book $24.95

Chord Studies for Electric Bass
by Rich Appleman
0-634-01646-6 Book $14.95

Reading Contemporary Electric Bass
by Rich Appleman
0-634-01338-6 Book $14.95

Rock Bass Lines
by Joe Santerre
0-634-01432-3 Book/CD $19.95

Slap Bass Lines
by Joe Santerre
0-634-02144-3 Book/CD $19.95

KEYBOARD

Solo Jazz Piano
by Neil Olmstead
0-634-00761-0 Book/CD $39.95

Hammond Organ Complete
by Dave Limina
0-634-01433-1 Book/CD $24.95

A Modern Method for Keyboard
by James Progris
0-634-01329-7 Vol. 1: Beginner
0-634-01330-0 Vol. 2: Intermediate
0-634-01830-2 Vol. 3: Advanced
Book $14.95 (each)

DRUMS AND PERCUSSION

Beyond the Backbeat
by Larry Finn
0-634-00701-7 Book/CD $19.95

Brazilian Rhythms for Drum Set and Percussion
By Alberto Netto
0-634-02143-5 Book/CD $29.95

Drum Set Warm-Ups
by Rod Morgenstein
0-634-00965-6 Book $12.95

Mastering the Art of Brushes
by Jon Hazilla
0-634-00962-1 Book/CD $19.95

The Reading Drummer
by Dave Vose
0-634-00961-3 Book $9.95

Rudiment Grooves for Drum Set
By Rick Considine
0-87639-009-2 Book/CD $19.95

SAXOPHONE

Books by Joseph Viola

Creative Reading Studies for Saxophone
0-634-01334-3 Book $14.95

Technique of the Saxophone
0-7935-5409-8 Volume 1: Scale Studies
0-7935-5412-8 Volume 2: Chord Studies
0-7935-5428-4 Volume 3: Rhythm Studies
Book $14.95 (each)

TOOLS FOR DJs

Turntable Technique:The Art of the DJ
by Stephen Webber
0-87639-010-6 Book/2-Record Set $34.95
0-87639-038-6 DVD $24.95
0-87639-039-4 VHS $24.95

Turntable Basics
by Stephen Webber
0-634-02612-7 Book $9.95

MUSIC BUSINESS

How to Get a Job in the Music & Recording Industry
by Keith Hatschek
0-634-01868-X Book $24.95

Mix Masters: Platinum Engineers Reveal Their Secrets for Success
by Maureen Droney
0-87639-019-X Book $24.95

The Musician's Internet
by Peter Spellman
0-634-03586-X Book $24.95

The New Music Therapist's Handbook, Second Edition
by Suzanne B. Hanser
0-634-00645-2 Book $29.95

The Self-Promoting Musician
by Peter Spellman
0-634-00644-4 Book $24.95

SONGWRITING / ARRANGING / VOICE

Arranging for Large Jazz Ensemble
by Ken Pullig
0-634-03656-4 Book/CD $39.95

Complete Guide to Film Scoring
by Richard Davis
0-634-00636-3 Book $24.95

The Contemporary Singer
By Anne Peckham
0-634-00797-1 Book/CD $24.95

Essential Ear Training
by Steve Prosser
0-634-00640-1 Book $14.95

Jazz Composition: Theory and Practice
By Ted Pease
0-87639-001-7 Book/CD $39.95

Melody in Songwriting
by Jack Perricone
0-634-00638-X Book $19.95

Modern Jazz Voicings
by Ted Pease and Ken Pullig
0-634-01443-9 Book/CD $24.95

Music Notation
by Mark McGrain
0-7935-0847-9 Book $19.95

Reharmonization Techn iques
by Randy Felts
0-634-01585-0 Book $29.95

The Songs of John Lennon
by John Stevens
0-634-01795-0 Book $24.95

The Songwriter's Workshop: Melody
by Jimmy Kachulis
0-634-02659-3 Book $24.95

Songwriting: Essential Guide to Lyric Form & Structure
by Pat Pattison
0-7935-1180-1 Book $14.95

Songwriting: Essential Guide to Rhyming
by Pat Pattison
0-7935-1181-X Book $14.95

BERKLEE PRACTICE METHOD

0-634-00650-9 **Bass** by Rich Appleman and John Repucci
0-634-00652-5 **Drum Set** by Ron Savage and Casey Scheuerell
0-634-00649-5 **Guitar** by Larry Baione
0-634-00651-7 **Keyboard** by Russell Hoffmann and Paul Schmeling
0-634-00795-5 **Alto Sax** by Jim Odgren and Bill Pierce
0-634-00798-0 **Tenor Sax** by Jim Odgren and Bill Pierce
0-634-00791-2 **Trombone** by Jeff Galindo
0-634-00790-4 **Trumpet** by Tiger Okoshi and Charles Lewis
0-634-00794-7 **Vibraphone** by Ed Saindon
0-634-00792-0 **Violin** by Matt Glaser and Mimi Rabson
Book/CD $14.95 (each)

BERKLEE INSTANT SERIES

0-634-01667-9 **Bass** by Danny Morris
0-634-02602-X **Drum Set** by Ron Savage
0-634-02951-7 **Guitar** by Tomo Fujita
0-634-03141-4 **Keyboard** by Paul Schmeling and Dave Limina
Book/CD $14.95 (each)

IMPROVISATION

Blues Improvisation Complete Series
by Jeff Harrington
0-634-01530-3 Bb Instruments
0-634-01532-X C Bass Instruments
0-634-00647-9 C Treble Instruments
0-634-01531-7 Eb Instruments
Book/CD $19.95 (each)

A Guide to Jazz Improvisation Series
by John LaPorta
0-634-00700-9 C Instruments
0-634-00762-9 Bb Instruments
0-634-00763-7 Eb Instruments
0-634-00764-5 Bass Clef
Book $16.95 (each)

MUSIC TECHNOLOGY

Arranging in the Digital World
by Corey Allen
0-634-00634-7 Book/MIDI Disk $19.95

Finale: An Easy Guide to Music Notation
by Tom Rudolph and Vince Leonard
0-634-01666-0 Book/CD-ROM $59.95

Producing in the Home Studio with Pro Tools Second Edition
by David Franz
0-87639-008-4 Book/CD-ROM $34.95

Recording in the Digital World
by Tom Rudolph and Vince Leonard
0-634-01324-6 Book $29.95

POP CULTURE

Inside the Hits
by Wayne Wadhams
0-634-01430-7 Book $29.95

Masters of Music: Conversations with Berklee Greats
by Mark Small and Andrew Taylor
0-634-00642-8 Book $24.95

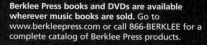